Understanding Diversity Comparative Insights into Global Education Systems

Rodrigo Tadeo

Copyright © [2023]

Title: Understanding Diversity Comparative Insights into Global Education Systems
Author's: Rodrigo Tadeo

This book was printed and published by [Publisher's: **Rodrigo Tadeo**] in [2023]

ISBN:

TABLE OF CONTENT

Chapter 4: Education Systems in North America 28

Chapter 6: Education Systems in Asia 60

Chapter 7: Education Systems in Africa 76

Chapter 10: Conclusion   119

Chapter 1: Introduction to Global Education Systems

The Importance of Understanding Diversity in Education

In today's rapidly changing world, understanding diversity in education is of utmost importance. As our societies become increasingly multicultural and interconnected, it is crucial to recognize and appreciate the diverse backgrounds, experiences, and perspectives of students and educators alike. This subchapter aims to shed light on the significance of embracing diversity in education, with a particular focus on comparative and international education.

One of the primary reasons why understanding diversity is crucial in education is that it fosters inclusivity and equality. By recognizing and celebrating the unique attributes of each individual, regardless of their race, ethnicity, religion, gender, or socioeconomic status, we create an environment that is conducive to learning and growth for all. Inclusive education ensures that every student feels valued, respected, and supported, enabling them to reach their full potential.

Moreover, understanding diversity in education promotes empathy and empathy in students. When students are exposed to diverse perspectives and cultures, they develop a broader understanding of the world and become more open-minded. This, in turn, cultivates empathy and tolerance, essential qualities for building a harmonious and inclusive society. By embracing diversity, we equip our students with the skills they need to navigate an increasingly globalized world.

Furthermore, understanding diversity in education allows for the exchange of ideas and knowledge across different cultures and educational systems. Comparative and international education is valuable for gaining insights into various educational approaches and systems worldwide. By studying the successes and challenges of different countries, educators can identify effective strategies and adapt them to their own context. This exchange of knowledge ensures continuous improvement and innovation in education.

Lastly, understanding diversity in education prepares students for the real world. In today's globalized workforce, individuals need to be able to collaborate with people from diverse backgrounds. By exposing students to diversity from an early age, we equip them with the skills necessary to thrive in a multicultural and interconnected world. Students learn to appreciate diversity, communicate effectively across cultures, and solve problems collectively.

In conclusion, understanding diversity in education is essential for creating inclusive and equitable learning environments, fostering empathy and tolerance, exchanging knowledge, and preparing students for the challenges of the real world. As educators, it is our responsibility to embrace and celebrate diversity in all its forms. By doing so, we contribute to the development of well-rounded individuals and a more harmonious and interconnected global society.

Objectives of the Book

"Understanding Diversity: Comparative Insights into Global Education Systems" aims to provide an in-depth exploration of the concept of diversity within the context of global education systems. This book is specifically written for a diverse audience, targeting individuals from all walks of life who are interested in comparative and international education.

The primary objective of this book is to foster a better understanding of the diverse education systems across the globe. It delves into the various educational practices, policies, and strategies implemented by different countries, acknowledging the unique challenges and opportunities they face. By examining these diverse systems, readers will gain valuable insights into how education is structured, delivered, and experienced in different parts of the world.

Another key objective is to highlight the importance of diversity in education. The book emphasizes the significant role that diversity plays in shaping educational outcomes and fostering inclusive learning environments. It explores the impact of cultural, linguistic, socioeconomic, and other forms of diversity on educational practices and outcomes. By doing so, it aims to promote a greater appreciation for diversity and its potential to enhance educational experiences.

Furthermore, this book seeks to encourage dialogue and collaboration among scholars, policymakers, educators, and other stakeholders in the field of comparative and international education. It provides a platform for sharing knowledge, experiences, and best practices from diverse educational contexts. By bringing together these insights, the book aims to contribute to the development of more effective and equitable education systems globally.

Overall, the objectives of "Understanding Diversity: Comparative Insights into Global Education Systems" are to:

1. Provide a comprehensive understanding of the diverse education systems across the globe.
2. Highlight the importance of diversity in education and its impact on educational practices and outcomes.
3. Foster appreciation for diversity and its potential to enhance educational experiences.
4. Facilitate dialogue and collaboration among scholars, policymakers, educators, and other stakeholders in the field of comparative and international education.
5. Contribute to the development of more effective and equitable education systems globally.

Through achieving these objectives, this book aims to contribute to the ongoing efforts towards creating inclusive, diverse, and high-quality education systems worldwide. It is a valuable resource for anyone interested in understanding and improving education on a global scale.

Methodology and Approach

In order to gain a comprehensive understanding of diversity in education systems around the world, this book employs a rigorous methodology and a multifaceted approach. By adopting a comparative and international education perspective, we aim to explore the various ways in which countries address diversity in their educational frameworks.

The methodology employed in this research is grounded in extensive literature review, data analysis, and case studies. We have delved into a wide range of scholarly works, including academic journals, books, reports, and policy documents, to gather a comprehensive understanding of the subject matter. This approach has allowed us to examine the diversity policies and practices implemented by different countries, as well as the outcomes and challenges associated with these approaches.

Furthermore, our methodology involves the analysis of a vast array of quantitative and qualitative data. By utilizing statistical data, we are able to identify patterns, trends, and disparities in educational outcomes and experiences across diverse populations. This quantitative analysis is supplemented by qualitative case studies, which provide in-depth insights into the lived experiences of students, teachers, and policymakers in diverse educational contexts. By combining these two approaches, we can paint a holistic picture of the complexities and nuances of diversity within global education systems.

The book's approach to understanding diversity is twofold: comparative and international. Through a comparative lens, we examine how different countries address and manage diversity within their education systems. By analyzing various policies, practices, and outcomes, we can identify innovative approaches and best practices that have proven successful in promoting inclusivity and equity. At the same time, the international dimension of our research allows us to explore cross-national perspectives on diversity, uncovering similarities, differences, and global trends in educational systems.

Addressed to a wide audience, including scholars, educators, policymakers, and students, this book aims to provide valuable insights into the field of comparative and international education. By examining diversity in education systems worldwide, we hope to foster a deeper understanding of the challenges and opportunities associated with educating diverse populations. Through an evidence-based approach, we seek to contribute to the development of effective policies and practices that promote inclusivity, equity, and excellence in education for all.

Chapter 2: Historical Perspectives on Education Systems

The Evolution of Education Systems

Education systems have undergone significant transformations throughout history, adapting to the changing needs of societies and the demands of an ever-evolving world. In this subchapter, we will explore the fascinating evolution of education systems and how they have shaped the world we live in today.

From ancient civilizations to modern-day societies, education has played a pivotal role in shaping individuals and communities. The earliest forms of education can be traced back to ancient civilizations such as Egypt, Mesopotamia, and China, where knowledge was primarily transmitted through oral traditions and apprenticeship models. These early systems primarily focused on imparting practical skills and transmitting cultural values from one generation to the next.

As societies progressed, formal education systems began to emerge. The ancient Greeks, for instance, established schools to educate citizens in subjects like mathematics, philosophy, and rhetoric. This intellectual tradition laid the foundation for the development of education systems in Europe and beyond.

The Industrial Revolution of the 18th and 19th centuries brought about significant changes in education. As societies became increasingly industrialized, schools shifted their focus to preparing individuals for the workforce. The rise of compulsory education and standardized curricula aimed to equip students with the skills needed for an industrialized society. This era also witnessed the advent of mass education, with schools becoming more accessible to a wider population.

In the 20th century, education systems underwent further transformations as societies grappled with social, political, and economic changes. The post-World War II era saw a rise in educational reforms across the globe, with governments recognizing the importance of education in nation-building and social development. Different models of education emerged, reflecting the values and priorities of each society. For instance, the United States emphasized a comprehensive education system, while countries like Finland focused on equity and holistic approaches.

With the advent of the digital age, education systems have once again evolved to meet the demands of a globalized and technologically advanced world. Online learning platforms, distance education, and the integration of technology in classrooms have become commonplace, providing new opportunities for students to access education and learn in innovative ways.

Understanding the evolution of education systems is crucial for comparative and international education scholars. By studying the historical context, societal influences, and policy decisions that have shaped education systems, we can gain valuable insights into the successes and challenges faced by different countries. This knowledge allows us to identify best practices, promote inclusive and equitable education, and foster cross-cultural understanding.

In conclusion, the evolution of education systems mirrors the progress of societies and reflects the changing needs of individuals and communities. From ancient civilizations to the digital age, education has been a cornerstone of human development. By understanding the past, we can pave the way for a brighter future in education for all.

Influences of Culture and Society on Education

Education is a fundamental aspect of every society and culture. It plays a crucial role in shaping individuals' knowledge, skills, and values, ultimately contributing to the development and progress of a nation. However, education is not a one-size-fits-all concept, as it is heavily influenced by the unique cultural and societal contexts in which it operates. Understanding these influences is vital for educators, policymakers, and researchers in the field of comparative and international education.

Culture, defined as the shared beliefs, values, customs, and behaviors of a particular group, significantly impacts the education system. Each culture has its own perspective on the purpose and goals of education. For example, in some societies, education is seen as a means to preserve and transmit traditional values and cultural heritage from one generation to another. In contrast, other cultures may prioritize education as a tool for social mobility and economic progress. These cultural differences shape the curriculum, teaching methods, and assessment strategies employed in schools.

Moreover, societal factors also exert a substantial influence on education. Socioeconomic status, gender norms, and political systems are among the key societal factors that shape educational practices. In societies with significant economic disparities, access to quality education may be limited for certain social groups, perpetuating social inequality. Similarly, gender norms can impact the opportunities and expectations placed on individuals, leading to disparities in educational attainment between genders.

Furthermore, the political system of a society plays a crucial role in determining the structure and policies of the education system. In some countries, education is centralized and tightly controlled by the government, ensuring a standardized curriculum and uniform teaching practices. Conversely, other nations may adopt a decentralized approach, allowing greater autonomy for schools and teachers to tailor education to local needs.

Understanding the influences of culture and society on education is essential for fostering inclusive and equitable educational systems worldwide. Comparative and international education research provides valuable insights into the strengths and weaknesses of different education systems, enabling policymakers to learn from successful practices and implement necessary reforms. By recognizing and embracing cultural diversity, education can become a powerful force for promoting social cohesion, intercultural understanding, and sustainable development.

In conclusion, the influences of culture and society on education are profound and multifaceted. Education is not a static entity but rather a dynamic reflection of the values, beliefs, and socio-political context of a society. Comparative and international education research contributes to our understanding of these influences, allowing us to create inclusive and effective education systems that cater to the needs of diverse populations. By recognizing the importance of culture and society in education, we can work towards a future where every individual has access to quality education and equal opportunities for personal and societal growth.

Key Milestones in Education Reforms

Education is an essential aspect of any society, shaping the future of individuals and communities. Throughout history, various key milestones have marked significant reforms in education systems worldwide. These milestones have aimed to address the evolving needs of learners, promote equality, and enhance educational outcomes. This subchapter explores some of the key milestones in education reforms that have shaped the landscape of global education systems.

One of the earliest milestones in education reforms can be attributed to the establishment of the first formal educational institutions. These institutions, such as ancient Greek academies and Islamic madrasas, laid the foundation for organized education systems. They emphasized the importance of knowledge acquisition and provided structured learning environments.

The Industrial Revolution in the 18th and 19th centuries brought about significant changes in society and education. This era witnessed the rise of public education systems, aiming to provide basic education to a larger population. The introduction of compulsory education laws in countries like Germany and the United States marked a major milestone in ensuring that education became accessible to all children, regardless of their social or economic background.

Another key milestone in education reforms was the advent of the progressive education movement in the late 19th and early 20th centuries. Led by influential educators such as John Dewey, this movement emphasized a child-centered approach to education. It promoted hands-on learning, critical thinking, and the integration of subjects, revolutionizing traditional teaching methods.

In the mid-20th century, the civil rights movement in the United States and other countries led to significant education reforms aimed at promoting equality and eliminating segregation. Landmark court cases, such as Brown v. Board of Education, mandated the desegregation of schools, ensuring that all students had equal access to quality education.

The late 20th and early 21st centuries witnessed a shift towards global cooperation and the recognition of the importance of education in achieving sustainable development. The Education for All (EFA) movement, launched in 1990, aimed to provide quality education to every child worldwide. This milestone highlighted the need for international collaboration and the development of global education goals.

In recent years, technological advancements have played a vital role in education reforms. The integration of digital technologies and online learning platforms has transformed traditional classroom settings, providing new opportunities for personalized learning and access to educational resources.

Understanding these key milestones in education reforms is crucial for policymakers, educators, and researchers in the field of comparative and international education. By analyzing the historical context and impact of these milestones, we can gain valuable insights into the factors shaping education systems worldwide. This knowledge can guide efforts to address current challenges, promote diversity, and foster inclusive and equitable education systems for all individuals, regardless of their backgrounds or circumstances.

Chapter 3: Comparative Framework for Analysis

Identifying Key Variables for Comparison

In the realm of Comparative and International Education, identifying key variables for comparison is a crucial step towards understanding the diversity that exists within global education systems. By examining various educational systems and their respective variables, we can gain valuable insights into the similarities and differences that shape educational practices around the world. This subchapter aims to provide a comprehensive overview of the key variables that researchers and educators alike should consider when comparing education systems.

One of the primary variables to consider is the structure and organization of education systems. This includes the division of educational levels, such as primary, secondary, and tertiary education, as well as the presence of specialized tracks or vocational programs. Understanding how education is structured in different countries allows for a deeper understanding of the pathways available to students and the implications this has on their educational experiences.

Another important variable to consider is the curriculum and content taught in schools. This includes subjects taught, teaching methods employed, and the presence of national or standardized curricula. By comparing curricula across different systems, we can gain insights into the priorities and values that underpin education in different countries.

The role of teachers and their qualifications is another key variable to consider. Understanding the qualifications required to become a teacher, the training they receive, and the level of autonomy they have in the classroom provides valuable insights into the quality of education and the level of professionalism within a system.

Other variables to consider include access to education, funding models, assessment practices, and the role of technology in the classroom. Each of these variables contributes to the overall understanding of a country's education system and its impact on learners.

By identifying and comparing these key variables, researchers and educators can gain a deeper understanding of the similarities and differences that exist between global education systems. This knowledge is invaluable for developing effective policies and practices that promote inclusive and equitable education worldwide.

Understanding Diversity: Comparative Insights into Global Education Systems aims to provide readers with the tools and knowledge necessary to navigate the complex landscape of comparative and international education. Through thorough analysis and exploration of key variables, this book seeks to foster a greater understanding of the diverse educational systems around the world, ultimately contributing to the advancement of education for all. Whether you are a researcher, educator, or simply interested in learning more about education systems, this book is a valuable resource that will broaden your perspective and deepen your understanding of the world of education.

Analytical Tools and Techniques

In today's interconnected world, understanding diversity is crucial for individuals, institutions, and societies. The field of Comparative and International Education offers valuable insights into global education systems, helping us recognize the diverse approaches and practices that exist worldwide. This subchapter, titled "Analytical Tools and Techniques," delves into the essential tools and techniques used to analyze and understand these systems effectively.

One of the fundamental analytical tools in Comparative and International Education is cross-national comparison. By comparing education systems across different countries, researchers can identify similarities, differences, and underlying patterns. This technique allows for a deeper understanding of how educational policies, practices, and outcomes vary across diverse contexts. Cross-national comparison helps us uncover the factors that contribute to the success or challenges faced by different education systems.

Another crucial analytical tool is the use of statistics and data analysis. Comparative and International Education relies heavily on quantitative research methods to provide evidence-based insights. Statistical analysis allows researchers to identify trends, measure the impact of policies, and evaluate the effectiveness of various educational interventions. By employing rigorous data analysis techniques, researchers can make informed decisions and recommendations to improve education systems globally.

Qualitative research methods also play a significant role in analyzing diversity in education systems. Approaches such as interviews, focus groups, and case studies provide valuable insights into the lived experiences of students, teachers, and policymakers. These methods help researchers understand the contextual factors that influence educational practices and outcomes. By combining qualitative and quantitative approaches, a comprehensive understanding of the complexities of global education systems can be achieved.

Analytical tools and techniques in Comparative and International Education also include policy analysis and evaluation. These tools allow researchers to critically examine educational policies, their implementation, and their impact on different student populations. By assessing the effectiveness of policies, researchers can provide recommendations for improvement and support evidence-based decision-making.

In conclusion, the subchapter on "Analytical Tools and Techniques" in Understanding Diversity: Comparative Insights into Global Education Systems provides valuable insights into how researchers in Comparative and International Education analyze and understand the diverse nature of education systems worldwide. Through the use of cross-national comparison, statistical analysis, qualitative research, and policy evaluation, researchers gain a comprehensive understanding of the complexities of education systems in different contexts. The knowledge gained from these analytical tools and techniques can help inform policies, practices, and interventions to promote inclusive and equitable education systems globally. This subchapter is relevant to anyone interested in understanding and contributing to the field of Comparative and International Education.

Challenges in Comparative Analysis

Comparative analysis is a valuable tool in understanding diversity in global education systems. By comparing different educational systems across countries, researchers can gain valuable insights into the strengths and weaknesses of various approaches, identify best practices, and learn from the experiences of others. However, conducting comparative analysis in the field of education is not without its challenges. In this subchapter, we will explore some of the key challenges that researchers and practitioners face when undertaking comparative analysis in the context of global education systems.

One of the primary challenges in comparative analysis is the vast diversity and complexity of education systems around the world. Each country has its unique cultural, social, and historical context that shapes its educational practices. It is crucial to acknowledge these differences and avoid making superficial comparisons that overlook the nuances of each system. Researchers must invest time and effort in understanding the underlying context and factors that contribute to the specificities of each education system.

Another challenge lies in the availability and reliability of data. While some countries have comprehensive and up-to-date data on their education systems, others may have limited or inconsistent data collection practices. Inaccurate or incomplete data can lead to biased or misleading comparisons. Researchers must exercise caution and ensure that they use reliable and comparable data sources to make meaningful comparisons.

Language and translation issues can also pose challenges in comparative analysis. Educational research and literature are often published in various languages, making it difficult to access and incorporate relevant studies from different countries. Additionally, translating educational terms and concepts accurately can be challenging, as they may not have direct equivalents in other languages. Researchers must be mindful of these linguistic barriers and make efforts to include a diverse range of sources in their analysis.

Moreover, comparative analysis requires a deep understanding of the cultural, political, and socio-economic factors that influence education systems. Researchers must be aware of their own biases and avoid imposing their perspectives on other countries' systems. It is essential to approach comparative analysis with an open mind and engage in collaborative discussions with local experts to gain a comprehensive understanding of the context.

In conclusion, conducting comparative analysis in the field of global education systems is a complex task that involves overcoming various challenges. Researchers must navigate the diversity and complexity of education systems, ensure the availability of reliable data, address language and translation barriers, and understand the underlying cultural and socio-economic factors. By acknowledging and addressing these challenges, researchers can make meaningful and insightful comparisons that contribute to a deeper understanding of the diverse approaches to education around the world.

Chapter 4: Education Systems in North America

Overview of Education Systems in the United States

Education is a cornerstone of society, shaping the future of individuals and nations. In the United States, the education system plays a crucial role in preparing students for various academic, professional, and personal pursuits. This subchapter provides an informative overview of the education systems in the United States, catering to an audience of "EVERY ONE" with a particular interest in comparative and international education.

The United States education system is decentralized, with education policies mainly determined at the state and local levels. However, the federal government also plays a significant role in setting broad goals, providing funding, and implementing regulations. The system is divided into three main levels: elementary, secondary, and post-secondary education.

Elementary education typically spans from kindergarten to fifth or sixth grade, depending on the state. It focuses on building foundational skills in subjects like mathematics, reading, writing, and science. The aim is to foster critical thinking, creativity, and social skills necessary for further educational and personal growth.

Secondary education in the United States encompasses middle school and high school. Middle school generally covers grades six to eight, while high school ranges from grades nine to twelve. The curriculum becomes more specialized, offering a range of subjects such as English, mathematics, science, history, and foreign languages. High school students can also choose elective courses based on their interests and career aspirations.

Post-secondary education in the United States is diverse and includes various options. Universities and colleges offer bachelor's, master's, and doctoral degree programs, providing students with a comprehensive education in fields such as arts, sciences, engineering, medicine, business, and more. Community colleges provide two-year associate degrees and vocational training programs, which are often more affordable and accessible alternatives to university education.

The United States education system also faces challenges such as funding disparities between schools in different regions, achievement gaps, and the need for equitable access to quality education for all students. Efforts are being made to address these issues through research, policy reforms, and innovative approaches to teaching and learning.

Understanding the education systems in the United States is crucial for comparative and international education scholars, policymakers, and practitioners. By exploring the strengths, weaknesses, and ongoing developments in the system, stakeholders can gain valuable insights to improve their own education systems and promote cross-cultural understanding.

In conclusion, this subchapter provides a comprehensive overview of the education systems in the United States, catering to an audience interested in comparative and international education. It highlights the decentralized nature of the system, the three main levels of education, and the challenges faced. By understanding the intricacies of the United States education system, individuals can contribute to the global discourse on education and work towards creating more inclusive and effective systems worldwide.

Structure and Organization

In any educational system, the structure and organization play a vital role in ensuring effective and efficient delivery of education to students. This subchapter delves into the importance of understanding the diverse structures and organizations of global education systems. It offers comparative insights into various education systems, providing valuable knowledge to individuals interested in comparative and international education.

The structure of an education system refers to the way it is organized, including the levels of schooling, the age groups served, and the progression from one level to the next. Understanding the different structures across countries can shed light on the strengths and weaknesses of each system. For example, some countries have a comprehensive system where all students follow a common curriculum until a certain age, while others have a more specialized system with different tracks or pathways available. By analyzing these structures, educators, policymakers, and researchers can gain a deeper understanding of the impact they have on student outcomes and educational equity.

Similarly, the organization of an education system encompasses the administrative and governance structures that support its functioning. This includes the roles and responsibilities of various stakeholders, such as government bodies, school boards, and teachers' unions. Exploring the organizational aspects of education systems allows us to examine the mechanisms in place for decision-making, resource allocation, and accountability. By comparing different organizational models, we can identify best practices and learn from successful systems.

This subchapter also explores how the structure and organization of education systems influence diversity and inclusivity. It examines how countries accommodate the needs of diverse student populations, including those from different cultural, linguistic, and socioeconomic backgrounds. By studying inclusive practices, we can gain insights into how education systems can promote social cohesion and ensure equal opportunities for all students.

Overall, this subchapter aims to provide a comprehensive understanding of the structure and organization of global education systems. By analyzing and comparing different models, readers will gain valuable insights into the strengths and weaknesses of diverse systems. This knowledge can inform policy decisions, improve educational practices, and contribute to the field of comparative and international education. Whether you are an educator, researcher, policymaker, or simply interested in understanding the complexities of education systems, this subchapter will provide valuable insights and broaden your perspective.

Curriculum and Assessment

Curriculum and Assessment: Nurturing Global Citizens through Education

In the ever-evolving landscape of education, the focus on curriculum and assessment plays a pivotal role in shaping the next generation of global citizens. This subchapter delves into the intricacies of curriculum development and assessment strategies, offering insights into the diverse approaches employed by educational systems worldwide.

The curriculum, as the backbone of any education system, serves as a roadmap for students' learning journey. However, the definition and content of curriculum vary significantly across countries, reflecting cultural, social, and economic contexts. Comparative and international education scholars have long recognized the importance of understanding these differences to foster effective educational policies and practices.

One key aspect of curriculum development is the consideration of diverse learners and their unique needs. Inclusive education, which embraces students from different backgrounds, abilities, and cultures, has emerged as a cornerstone of modern curricula. This subchapter explores the ways in which educational systems around the world strive to create inclusive environments by promoting diversity, equity, and social justice.

Furthermore, assessment practices are closely linked to curriculum and play a vital role in measuring student progress and achievement. Traditional assessment methods, such as standardized tests, have faced criticism for their limited ability to capture the complexity of learning outcomes. As a result, alternative approaches, including project-based assessments, portfolios, and self-assessment, have gained traction in many educational systems. This subchapter examines the advantages and challenges associated with different assessment methods, shedding light on how they reflect a country's educational priorities and values.

Moreover, the subchapter highlights the increasing emphasis on global competence in curricula and assessments. In an interconnected world, students need more than just academic knowledge; they require skills such as critical thinking, problem-solving, intercultural communication, and empathy. Comparative insights into how countries incorporate global competence in their educational frameworks provide valuable lessons for educators and policymakers aiming to prepare students for a rapidly changing global society.

Ultimately, this subchapter on curriculum and assessment seeks to foster a deeper understanding of the diverse approaches to education worldwide. By examining the interplay between curricula and assessment strategies, it aims to inspire dialogue and collaboration among educators, researchers, and policymakers, leading to the development of inclusive, relevant, and effective educational systems that nurture the potential of every learner, regardless of their background or nationality.

Teacher Training and Professional Development

In the fast-paced and ever-evolving field of education, it is imperative that teachers continuously enhance their skills and knowledge to effectively meet the needs of a diverse student population. Teacher training and professional development play a vital role in ensuring that educators remain competent and capable of providing quality education to students. This subchapter delves into the significance of teacher training and professional development in the context of comparative and international education.

Teacher training programs serve as the foundation for preparing new teachers to enter the classroom. These programs equip aspiring educators with the necessary pedagogical knowledge, instructional strategies, and classroom management skills. They also provide opportunities for pre-service teachers to engage in practical experiences such as student teaching, internships, or practicums, which allow them to apply theory into practice. By exposing future teachers to diverse teaching methods and educational philosophies, teacher training programs foster an inclusive and well-rounded approach to education.

Additionally, ongoing professional development is essential for experienced teachers to stay updated with the latest research, methodologies, and technologies in the field of education. In an era where technology is rapidly changing the way we live and learn, teachers need to adapt and incorporate these advancements into their teaching practices. Professional development workshops, conferences, and seminars provide opportunities for teachers to engage in collaborative learning, share best practices, and gain new insights into effective teaching strategies.

Furthermore, teacher training and professional development should address the important aspects of diversity and inclusion. In today's globalized world, classrooms are becoming increasingly multicultural and diverse. Teachers need to be equipped with the knowledge and skills to create inclusive and culturally sensitive learning environments. Training programs and professional development initiatives should emphasize the importance of understanding and valuing different cultures, languages, and learning styles. By doing so, teachers can effectively cater to the needs of diverse learners and promote equity and equality in education.

In conclusion, teacher training and professional development are crucial components of a successful education system. They ensure that teachers are well-prepared to meet the challenges of a diverse student population and are equipped with the necessary skills and knowledge to provide quality education. By investing in teacher training and professional development, societies can foster an inclusive, equitable, and culturally sensitive approach to education, ultimately leading to positive outcomes for all students.

Education Systems in Canada

Canada is renowned for its high-quality education system, which consistently ranks among the top performers globally. With its commitment to diversity and inclusive education, Canada provides a unique and enriching learning environment for students of all backgrounds. This subchapter explores the education systems in Canada, offering a comprehensive understanding of its structure, policies, and key features.

The Canadian education system is decentralized, with each province and territory having the authority to develop and manage its own education policies. However, there are several commonalities across the country, such as mandatory education, a focus on bilingualism, and a commitment to equity and accessibility.

In Canada, education is compulsory for children aged 6 to 16, ensuring that every child has access to education. The system is divided into different levels: elementary, secondary, and post-secondary. Elementary education typically covers grades 1 to 8, while secondary education comprises grades 9 to 12. Post-secondary education includes universities, colleges, and vocational institutions, offering a wide range of academic and professional programs.

One of the notable strengths of the Canadian education system is its commitment to bilingualism. English and French are the official languages of Canada, and students have the opportunity to learn and study in both languages. French immersion programs are available across the country, allowing students to learn French as a second language and develop a greater understanding and appreciation for Canada's linguistic and cultural diversity.

Moreover, Canada's education system places a strong emphasis on equity and accessibility. The government strives to provide equal opportunities for all students, regardless of their socio-economic background, ethnicity, or abilities. Inclusive education is a core principle, ensuring that students with disabilities or special needs receive appropriate support and accommodations to fully participate in the educational experience.

Another noteworthy aspect of the Canadian education system is its focus on critical thinking, creativity, and innovation. The curriculum encourages students to develop problem-solving skills, think independently, and engage in collaborative learning. This approach fosters the development of well-rounded individuals who are equipped to contribute meaningfully to society.

In conclusion, the education systems in Canada offer a comprehensive and inclusive learning experience for students of all ages and backgrounds. With its commitment to bilingualism, equity, and accessibility, Canada has established a reputation as a global leader in education. By understanding the key features of the Canadian education system, educators, policymakers, and researchers in the field of Comparative and International Education can gain valuable insights to enhance their own educational practices and systems.

Structure and Organization

In today's interconnected world, understanding the diversity that exists in global education systems is crucial. This subchapter titled "Structure and Organization" explores the various structures and organizational features found in different education systems around the world.

The structure of an education system refers to how it is organized, including the levels of education, the curriculum, and the administrative hierarchy. Each country has its own unique structure, influenced by historical, cultural, and social factors. By examining these structures, we can gain valuable insights into the similarities and differences between education systems and how they shape the learning experiences of students.

One key aspect of structure and organization is the different levels of education within a system. Some countries have a three-tiered structure consisting of primary, secondary, and tertiary education, while others may have additional levels or variations in the age ranges covered. Understanding these levels helps us grasp the progression of students through the education system and the different goals and expectations at each stage.

Another important consideration is the curriculum. The content taught in schools varies greatly between countries, reflecting the values, priorities, and cultural heritage of each nation. Comparative and international education scholars analyze these curricula to examine the similarities and differences in educational content and to assess how well they prepare students for their futures.

The administrative hierarchy within education systems also plays a vital role in their structure and organization. This includes the roles of ministries, departments of education, school boards, and other governing bodies. Understanding the power dynamics and decision-making processes within these structures is essential for identifying who holds authority and influence over education policy and practice.

By delving into the intricacies of structure and organization, we can gain a comprehensive understanding of how education systems function globally. This knowledge is indispensable for policymakers, educators, researchers, and anyone interested in comparative and international education. It allows us to identify best practices, learn from successful models, and address challenges faced by different education systems.

In conclusion, this subchapter on "Structure and Organization" provides valuable insights into the diverse ways in which education systems are structured and organized worldwide. By exploring the levels of education, curriculum, and administrative hierarchies, we can deepen our understanding of the similarities and differences between global education systems. This knowledge is essential for enhancing educational practices, promoting equity, and fostering cooperation in the field of comparative and international education.

Curriculum and Assessment

Curriculum and Assessment: Nurturing Diversity in Education

Education systems across the globe are constantly evolving to meet the needs of an increasingly diverse and interconnected world. In this subchapter, we delve into the critical aspects of curriculum and assessment, exploring how these components shape educational experiences and foster inclusivity in comparative and international education.

Curriculum, as the backbone of any education system, plays a pivotal role in imparting knowledge, skills, and values to learners. However, a one-size-fits-all approach is no longer viable in today's multicultural societies. Recognizing this, educational policymakers are embracing curriculum frameworks that celebrate diversity and promote cultural understanding. By incorporating diverse perspectives, histories, and experiences, curricula can empower students to appreciate and respect different cultures, fostering global citizenship.

Inclusive curricula also address the educational needs of marginalized groups, ensuring that their voices are heard and their experiences are validated. By providing culturally responsive materials and pedagogical approaches, educators can create safe and inclusive spaces where students from all backgrounds can thrive. Moreover, the inclusion of diverse narratives in the curriculum can challenge stereotypes, biases, and prejudices, promoting tolerance, empathy, and social cohesion.

Assessment, as an integral part of the educational process, must also adapt to the principles of diversity and inclusivity. Standardized tests, which often favor certain cultural or socioeconomic groups, can perpetuate inequalities and hinder the development of a diverse and equitable society. Instead, educators and policymakers are exploring alternative assessment methods that value multiple forms of intelligence, creativity, and critical thinking. Performance-based assessments, portfolios, and project-based evaluations allow students to demonstrate their knowledge and skills in various ways, accommodating their unique strengths and learning styles.

In addition, assessment practices should consider cultural and linguistic diversity, ensuring that language barriers do not impede students' ability to showcase their true capabilities. Culturally responsive assessments provide accommodations and support for learners from diverse backgrounds, allowing them to express their knowledge and skills effectively.

By embracing inclusive curriculum and assessment practices, educators can create learning environments that celebrate diversity, promote social justice, and prepare students for a globalized world. However, ensuring the successful implementation of these practices requires ongoing professional development and collaborations among educators, policymakers, and the wider community.

In conclusion, curriculum and assessment are essential components of comparative and international education. By recognizing and valuing diversity, educational systems can cultivate inclusive environments, nurture global citizens, and foster social harmony. Through ongoing research, dialogue, and collaboration, we can continue to refine our approaches, ensuring that every learner receives an education that respects and celebrates their unique identities and experiences.

Teacher Training and Professional Development

In the ever-evolving landscape of education, one constant remains: the critical role of teachers in shaping the minds of future generations. Teacher training and professional development have emerged as indispensable components in ensuring the delivery of quality education worldwide. This subchapter explores the importance of teacher training and professional development in the context of comparative and international education.

Teacher training programs play a pivotal role in equipping educators with the necessary skills and knowledge to deliver effective instruction. These programs offer a comprehensive understanding of pedagogical approaches, curriculum design, and classroom management techniques. By instilling a strong foundation in these areas, teacher training programs empower educators to create engaging and inclusive learning environments.

Professional development, on the other hand, is an ongoing process that allows teachers to continuously refine their skills and stay abreast of the latest educational trends and best practices. It enables educators to deepen their subject knowledge, develop innovative teaching methods, and enhance their ability to cater to the diverse needs of students. Professional development opportunities can take various forms, including workshops, conferences, online courses, and collaboration with colleagues.

One key aspect of teacher training and professional development in comparative and international education is the promotion of diversity and inclusion. As societies become increasingly diverse, teachers must be prepared to meet the unique needs of students from various cultural, linguistic, and socioeconomic backgrounds. By incorporating diversity and inclusion into teacher training and professional development programs, educators can foster inclusive classrooms where every student feels valued and supported.

Moreover, teacher training and professional development also play a critical role in addressing educational inequalities across different countries and regions. By investing in training programs that are tailored to the specific needs of local communities, policymakers can bridge the gap between well-resourced and under-resourced schools. This approach ensures that all students, regardless of their socioeconomic background or geographic location, have access to high-quality education.

In conclusion, teacher training and professional development are vital components of comparative and international education. These initiatives empower educators to deliver quality education, promote diversity and inclusion, and address educational inequalities. By investing in the continuous growth and development of teachers, we can create a brighter future for our global education systems and the students they serve.

Chapter 5: Education Systems in Europe

Overview of Education Systems in the United Kingdom

Education is a fundamental pillar of any society, shaping the future of individuals and the nation as a whole. The United Kingdom has a rich history of education, known for its diverse and comprehensive systems that have influenced education worldwide. In this subchapter, we will provide an overview of the education systems in the United Kingdom, highlighting their unique features and contributions to comparative and international education.

The United Kingdom is comprised of four distinct countries: England, Scotland, Wales, and Northern Ireland. Each country has its own education system, governed by separate policies and regulations, while also adhering to overarching national frameworks. This diversity reflects the historical and cultural differences within the UK.

In England, the education system is divided into four key stages: Early Years Foundation Stage (ages 3-5), Primary Education (ages 5-11), Secondary Education (ages 11-16), and Post-16 Education (ages 16+). Students in England follow a national curriculum that provides a standardized framework for learning.

Scotland's education system also follows a similar structure, although there are distinct differences. For instance, in Scotland, primary education starts at age 4, and there is an additional year of secondary education, making it a six-year program. Scottish education places a strong emphasis on local authority control and flexibility in the curriculum.

In Wales, education is organized into Foundation Phase (ages 3-7), Key Stage 2 (ages 7-11), Key Stage 3 (ages 11-14), Key Stage 4 (ages 14-16), and Post-16 Education. Welsh education is characterized by its commitment to bilingualism, with English and Welsh being core subjects.

Northern Ireland's education system is similar to that of England, with primary and secondary education following the same structure. However, Northern Ireland has a separate curriculum that reflects its unique history and cultural context.

The education systems in the United Kingdom share some common features, such as national assessments, teacher training programs, and quality assurance mechanisms. However, they also exhibit significant differences in terms of governance, curriculum, and assessment practices.

Understanding the education systems in the United Kingdom provides valuable insights for comparative and international education research. By exploring these systems, researchers can gain a deeper understanding of the diverse approaches and strategies employed in different countries, enabling them to identify best practices and challenges that may be applicable to other national contexts.

In conclusion, the education systems in the United Kingdom offer a rich and diverse landscape for study and comparison. Whether you are an educator, researcher, or simply interested in understanding education systems around the world, exploring the intricacies of the United Kingdom's education systems will provide valuable insights into comparative and international education.

Structure and Organization

In the ever-changing landscape of global education systems, understanding the structure and organization of these systems is crucial for policymakers, educators, and students alike. This subchapter aims to provide comparative insights into the diverse educational structures and organizations around the world, catering to the interests of a wide range of readers, including those in the field of Comparative and International Education.

One of the most critical aspects of any education system is its structure. This refers to the way educational institutions are organized, from primary schools to universities, and the various levels and pathways available to students. By examining different educational structures, we can gain a deeper understanding of the strengths and weaknesses of each system and identify potential areas for improvement.

Furthermore, this subchapter explores how education systems are organized in different countries, taking into account factors such as government policies, cultural values, and socio-economic conditions. By comparing and contrasting these systems, we can examine the impact of these factors on educational outcomes and identify best practices that can be adopted in other contexts.

Additionally, this subchapter delves into the organization of educational institutions themselves. It explores topics such as school governance, leadership structures, and curriculum development. By examining these aspects, we can gain insights into how schools and universities are managed and how decisions are made at various levels of the education system.

Moreover, this subchapter addresses the role of international organizations, such as UNESCO and the World Bank, in shaping the structure and organization of education systems worldwide. It discusses the initiatives and policies introduced by these organizations to promote access, equity, and quality in education globally.

Finally, this subchapter highlights the importance of understanding the structure and organization of education systems in fostering inclusive and equitable learning environments. By recognizing the diverse needs and backgrounds of students, educators can design educational structures that accommodate these differences and ensure that every learner has an equal opportunity to succeed.

Whether you are an educator, policymaker, or student interested in Comparative and International Education, this subchapter provides valuable insights into the structure and organization of education systems worldwide. By examining different approaches and best practices, we can work towards creating more inclusive and effective educational systems that meet the needs of diverse learners.

Curriculum and Assessment

In the realm of education, the concepts of curriculum and assessment are pivotal in shaping the learning experiences of students across the globe. The subchapter "Curriculum and Assessment" delves into the intricacies of these two interconnected aspects, offering a comprehensive understanding of their significance in the field of comparative and international education.

Curriculum, the backbone of any education system, encompasses the knowledge, skills, and values that are deemed essential for students to acquire during their educational journey. This subchapter explores how curricula vary across different global education systems, taking into account cultural, social, and economic factors that shape educational priorities. By examining diverse curricular models, readers will gain insights into the strengths and weaknesses of various approaches, allowing for a more nuanced understanding of how different countries strive to prepare their students for the challenges of the modern world.

Assessment, on the other hand, plays a crucial role in measuring student learning and progress. This subchapter highlights the various assessment methods employed in different education systems, including standardized tests, performance-based assessments, and portfolio assessments. By examining the advantages and disadvantages of these assessment approaches, readers will gain a deeper understanding of how assessment practices can influence teaching and learning outcomes.

Moreover, the subchapter delves into the ongoing debates surrounding curriculum and assessment, such as the tension between standardized testing and promoting creativity, critical thinking, and problem-solving skills. It examines the impact of high-stakes testing on students, teachers, and educational systems, shedding light on potential alternatives and innovative assessment practices that foster a more holistic understanding of student capabilities.

The subchapter also explores how curriculum and assessment are influenced by broader educational policies, including national education goals, accountability systems, and teacher training programs. By examining the interplay between policy and practice, readers will gain insights into how curriculum and assessment decisions are made and implemented at various levels of the education system.

Overall, this subchapter provides a comprehensive overview of curriculum and assessment in comparative and international education. It equips readers with the necessary knowledge and tools to critically analyze and evaluate curricular and assessment practices across different education systems, fostering a deeper understanding of the complexities and challenges faced by educators worldwide. Whether you are an educator, policymaker, or simply interested in understanding the intricacies of global education systems, this subchapter offers valuable insights into the ever-evolving landscape of curriculum and assessment.

Teacher Training and Professional Development

In the ever-evolving landscape of education, it is crucial for teachers to continuously update their skills and knowledge to meet the diverse needs of students. This subchapter explores the importance of teacher training and professional development in the field of comparative and international education.

Teacher training programs play a pivotal role in equipping educators with the necessary tools to effectively engage with students from diverse backgrounds. These programs provide teachers with a solid foundation in pedagogical techniques, content knowledge, and classroom management strategies. A well-designed teacher training program not only focuses on theoretical concepts but also emphasizes practical applications in real-world classroom settings.

Professional development further enhances the skills and expertise of teachers throughout their careers. It offers opportunities for educators to refine their instructional practices, learn about emerging educational trends, and collaborate with colleagues from different cultural and educational backgrounds. Through workshops, conferences, and online courses, teachers can stay up-to-date with the latest research and best practices in teaching and learning.

One of the key objectives of teacher training and professional development is to foster inclusive education. In an increasingly diverse world, teachers need to be equipped with the knowledge and skills to create inclusive learning environments that celebrate the uniqueness of each student. Training programs should focus on cultural sensitivity, understanding and addressing biases, and implementing inclusive teaching strategies. By promoting diversity and inclusion, teachers can help students develop empathy, respect, and appreciation for different cultures and perspectives.

Effective teacher training and professional development programs also recognize the importance of continuous assessment and feedback. Teachers should have access to ongoing support and evaluation to identify areas for improvement and receive guidance for their professional growth. Collaborative learning communities, mentorship programs, and peer observations can provide valuable opportunities for teachers to reflect on their practice and refine their teaching strategies.

In conclusion, teacher training and professional development are essential components of a comprehensive education system. By investing in the continuous growth and development of teachers, we can ensure that classrooms are inclusive, engaging, and responsive to the diverse needs of students. Through ongoing training and support, educators can adapt to the changing educational landscape and make a positive impact on the lives of learners worldwide.

Education Systems in Germany

Germany is renowned for its strong and well-structured education system, which has played a significant role in shaping the country's economic success and social development. With a focus on equal opportunities and a commitment to providing high-quality education for all, Germany's education system serves as an exemplary model for many countries around the world.

The German education system is divided into four main levels: early childhood education, primary education, secondary education, and tertiary education. Early childhood education, also known as Kindergarten, is not compulsory but is highly encouraged and provides a foundation for children's social, emotional, and cognitive development before they enter primary school.

Primary education starts at the age of six and lasts for four years. It serves as a fundamental stage where students acquire basic literacy, numeracy, and social skills. After completing primary education, students progress to secondary education, which is divided into two tracks: the Gymnasium and the Gesamtschule.

The Gymnasium is an academic track that prepares students for higher education and typically lasts for nine years. It is highly selective, and students must meet certain academic standards to gain admission. The Gesamtschule, on the other hand, offers a comprehensive education that combines both academic and vocational training. It caters to students of varying abilities and provides more flexibility in terms of subject choices.

After completing secondary education, students can choose to pursue tertiary education at universities, technical colleges, or vocational schools. Germany is known for its strong vocational education and training (VET) system, which provides practical skills and prepares students for the job market. Tertiary education is highly valued in Germany, and universities offer a wide range of programs in various fields, both in German and English.

One unique aspect of the German education system is its emphasis on equal opportunities and providing free education for all students, including international students. Additionally, the system promotes social mobility by offering financial support, such as scholarships and grants, to students from disadvantaged backgrounds.

In conclusion, the education system in Germany is highly regarded for its commitment to equal opportunities and the provision of high-quality education for all. With a well-structured framework that emphasizes both academic and vocational training, Germany's education system serves as a benchmark for many countries seeking to enhance their own educational practices.

Structure and Organization

In the realm of education, structure and organization play a pivotal role in shaping the quality and effectiveness of learning systems. Understanding how different education systems are structured and organized is crucial for anyone interested in comparative and international education. This subchapter aims to provide insights into the diverse ways education systems are structured and organized worldwide, shedding light on the factors that contribute to their successes and challenges.

One fundamental aspect of structure and organization in education is the division of levels and stages of learning. Education systems vary in terms of the number and organization of these levels. Some countries have a three-tiered system, consisting of primary, secondary, and tertiary education, while others may have a four-tiered system, including early childhood education as the initial stage. By exploring the organization of these tiers, readers will gain a deeper understanding of how education systems prepare students for future academic and professional endeavors.

Furthermore, this subchapter delves into the organization of curriculum and instructional methodologies across different education systems. While some countries adopt a centralized curriculum, others may grant more autonomy to individual schools or teachers. The way in which subjects are taught and assessed also varies, with some systems emphasizing standardized testing and others favoring project-based assessments. By examining these differences, readers will gain a nuanced understanding of how curriculum and instruction shape the educational experiences of students worldwide.

Additionally, this subchapter explores the organizational structures of educational institutions, such as schools and universities. It discusses the different models of governance and administration employed in various countries, including both centralized and decentralized approaches. Readers will gain insights into the roles and responsibilities of key stakeholders within these institutions, such as principals, teachers, and governing bodies.

Understanding the structure and organization of education systems is crucial for addressing the challenges and opportunities that arise in today's globalized world. By comparing and contrasting different models, readers can identify best practices and innovative approaches that can be adopted or adapted to enhance their own education systems. Whether you are an educator, policymaker, or simply curious about the world of education, this subchapter will equip you with valuable knowledge to navigate the complexities of comparative and international education.

Curriculum and Assessment

Curriculum and Assessment: Shaping Global Education Systems

In the ever-changing landscape of education, the design and implementation of curriculum and assessment play a crucial role in shaping the learning experiences of students worldwide. These essential components of any education system are the backbone upon which teaching and learning are built. In this subchapter, we delve into the intricacies of curriculum and assessment in the context of comparative and international education, exploring their significance and impact on diverse populations.

Curriculum refers to the planned and organized set of knowledge, skills, and experiences that students are expected to acquire during their educational journey. It serves as a roadmap, guiding educators in providing a comprehensive and well-rounded education to students. However, the content and structure of curricula vary significantly across countries, reflecting diverse cultural, social, and economic contexts. Understanding these differences is vital for comparative and international education researchers, policymakers, and practitioners to ensure equitable and inclusive education for all.

Assessment, on the other hand, is the process of evaluating students' learning outcomes and progress. It serves multiple purposes, including measuring achievement, diagnosing areas of improvement, and guiding instruction. However, assessments can also perpetuate inequalities if they fail to consider diverse cultural, linguistic, and socio-economic backgrounds of students. In this subchapter, we explore how assessment practices can be culturally sensitive, inclusive, and fair, thereby promoting educational equity.

By examining a range of global education systems, we gain insights into how different countries approach curriculum development and assessment methodologies. We analyze the challenges and opportunities inherent in these systems, exploring innovative practices and successful strategies that can be adapted and implemented across borders. Furthermore, this subchapter highlights the importance of continuous evaluation and adaptation of curriculum and assessment approaches to meet the evolving needs of students in an increasingly interconnected world.

For researchers in comparative and international education, this subchapter offers a comprehensive overview of curriculum and assessment frameworks, enabling them to identify patterns, trends, and best practices from around the globe. Policymakers can draw inspiration from successful models, adapting and tailoring them to their specific contexts. Educators and practitioners will find valuable insights for designing inclusive curricula and implementing effective assessment strategies that promote diversity, foster critical thinking, and prepare students for the challenges of the 21st century.

In conclusion, the subchapter on Curriculum and Assessment provides a holistic understanding of the global education landscape. It emphasizes the importance of acknowledging and embracing diversity in curricula and assessment practices to ensure equitable and inclusive education for all learners. By exploring and comparing these essential components, we can work towards building a more harmonious and effective educational system that celebrates the uniqueness of every learner.

Teacher Training and Professional Development

In today's rapidly changing world, education systems across the globe are facing unprecedented challenges. The demand for inclusive and equitable education is growing, necessitating a well-prepared and diverse teaching workforce. This subchapter, titled "Teacher Training and Professional Development," delves into the critical aspects of preparing teachers for the demands of the 21st-century classroom, with a focus on comparative and international education.

Teacher training and professional development play a pivotal role in shaping the quality of education systems worldwide. As the need for skilled and adaptable educators increases, countries must invest in comprehensive training programs that equip teachers with the necessary knowledge and skills to meet the diverse needs of their students. This subchapter explores how different countries approach teacher training, highlighting both successful strategies and areas for improvement.

One key theme within teacher training is the importance of understanding diversity. In an increasingly globalized world, classrooms are becoming more diverse, both in terms of cultural backgrounds and learning needs. Effective teacher training programs provide educators with the tools to address this diversity, fostering inclusive and culturally responsive learning environments.

Furthermore, this subchapter examines the role of professional development in supporting teachers' ongoing growth and learning. Professional development programs enable educators to stay abreast of emerging educational practices, technologies, and research. They also facilitate collaboration and networking among teachers, promoting a culture of continuous improvement within education systems.

The subchapter also delves into the challenges and opportunities presented by technology in teacher training and professional development. With the rapid advancement of digital tools and online platforms, educators have access to a wealth of resources and opportunities for virtual collaboration. However, this also poses challenges, such as ensuring equitable access to technology and promoting critical digital literacy skills among teachers.

In conclusion, "Teacher Training and Professional Development" is a subchapter that explores the critical role of preparing and supporting teachers in the context of comparative and international education. It highlights the importance of understanding diversity, the need for ongoing professional development, and the opportunities and challenges presented by technology. By investing in comprehensive and inclusive training programs, countries can ensure that their education systems are equipped to meet the diverse needs of learners in the 21st century. This subchapter provides valuable insights and recommendations for policymakers, educators, and researchers interested in improving the quality of education worldwide.

Chapter 6: Education Systems in Asia

Overview of Education Systems in China

China, with its rich history and fast-paced development, has become a global leader in various aspects, including its education system. Understanding the education system in China provides valuable insights into the country's cultural and social dynamics, as well as its commitment to academic excellence.

The education system in China is highly centralized, with the Ministry of Education playing a key role in policy-making and regulation. It consists of three main stages: primary education, secondary education, and higher education. Primary education, which is compulsory and lasts for six years, focuses on building a solid foundation in Chinese language, mathematics, and science.

Secondary education is divided into lower and upper secondary levels. The lower secondary level, also known as junior high school, lasts for three years and emphasizes a broad range of subjects, including foreign languages, history, and physical education. At the upper secondary level, students can choose between academic or vocational tracks. The academic track prepares students for the national college entrance examination, known as the Gaokao, which determines admission into higher education institutions.

Higher education in China is highly valued and competitive. Universities and colleges offer a wide range of programs in various fields, and admission is based on students' Gaokao scores. Chinese universities have made significant progress in recent years and are increasingly being recognized globally for their research contributions and academic excellence.

It is important to note that China's education system places a strong emphasis on discipline, rote memorization, and standardized testing. While this approach has its benefits in terms of fostering discipline and providing a clear path for academic achievement, it has also been criticized for stifling creativity and individuality.

In recent years, the Chinese government has recognized the need for educational reforms, aiming to foster a more holistic and student-centered approach. Efforts have been made to reduce the emphasis on standardized testing and promote critical thinking, creativity, and innovation in the classroom.

Understanding the education systems in China provides valuable insights into the country's culture, values, and aspirations. It also offers comparative perspectives for educators and policymakers interested in international education systems. By examining the strengths and weaknesses of different education systems, we can identify best practices and adapt them to our own contexts, ultimately working towards improving education worldwide.

Structure and Organization

In the vast landscape of global education systems, understanding the structure and organization of different systems is crucial for gaining insights into the diverse ways in which education is delivered across the world. This subchapter delves into the intricacies of education systems, providing valuable comparative insights into the field of global education.

One of the fundamental aspects of any education system is its structure. Education systems can be organized in various ways, depending on cultural, historical, and political factors. This subchapter explores different models of organization, ranging from centralized systems where decisions are made at the national level, to decentralized systems where power is devolved to local authorities. By examining the advantages and disadvantages of each model, readers will gain a deeper understanding of the impact of organizational structures on educational outcomes.

Furthermore, this subchapter delves into the organizational aspects within education systems. It explores the role of ministries of education, educational boards, and other governing bodies in shaping and implementing educational policies. Understanding the dynamics of these organizations is crucial for comprehending the decision-making processes that drive education systems. Readers will gain insights into the challenges faced by these organizations, such as ensuring equity and quality in education, fostering innovation, and adapting to societal changes.

The subchapter also sheds light on the role of teachers and school leaders within the organizational structure of education systems. It explores the ways in which educators are trained, supported, and evaluated, and how their roles contribute to the overall success of the system. By comparing different approaches to teacher training and professional development, readers will gain a comprehensive understanding of the importance of investing in the teaching profession for achieving educational excellence.

Ultimately, this subchapter aims to provide readers with a holistic view of the structure and organization of global education systems. By examining various models, organizations, and roles within education systems, readers will be able to critically analyze and compare different approaches. This knowledge will not only benefit those interested in the field of comparative and international education, but also anyone seeking to understand the complexities and nuances of education systems around the world.

Curriculum and Assessment

Curriculum and Assessment: Nurturing Diversity in Global Education Systems

In the realm of education, the curriculum and assessment frameworks adopted by different countries play a crucial role in shaping the educational experiences of students. Understanding the nuances of curriculum design and assessment practices across diverse global education systems is essential for fostering a comprehensive and inclusive learning environment. This subchapter delves into the intricacies of curriculum and assessment, exploring how various countries approach these aspects and the impact they have on students' learning outcomes.

Curriculum, at its core, is a blueprint that outlines the knowledge, skills, and competencies that students are expected to acquire during their educational journey. It serves as a guide for teachers, students, and policymakers, providing a structured framework for learning. However, the content and structure of curricula can vary significantly across countries, reflecting the unique cultural, social, and economic contexts in which education systems operate.

In this subchapter, we explore the diverse approaches to curriculum design and the underlying philosophies that shape them. We examine how countries strike a balance between standardized national curricula and the need to accommodate regional and local contexts. Additionally, we delve into the role of stakeholders, such as teachers, students, parents, and community members, in shaping the curriculum to reflect their values and aspirations.

Assessment, on the other hand, is the means through which students' learning and progress are measured. It encompasses a range of tools and methods, including tests, exams, projects, and portfolios. The subchapter delves into the various assessment practices employed by different education systems, highlighting the objectives they aim to achieve and the challenges they may face.

We discuss the role of assessment in promoting inclusive education, considering how it can be adapted to accommodate students with diverse learning needs and abilities. We explore alternative assessment methods that focus on a more holistic evaluation of students' skills and competencies, going beyond traditional standardized tests. Furthermore, we analyze the potential biases and inequities inherent in assessment practices and propose strategies for mitigating these challenges.

By understanding the diversity in curriculum and assessment practices across global education systems, educators, policymakers, and researchers can gain valuable insights into what works and what can be improved. This subchapter aims to equip readers with a comparative understanding of curriculum and assessment, facilitating the exchange of ideas and best practices in comparative and international education. Ultimately, it is through this understanding that we can foster educational systems that embrace and nurture the diversity of learners, ensuring equitable and inclusive educational opportunities for all.

Teacher Training and Professional Development

In any education system, teachers play a crucial role in shaping the minds and future of our society. They are responsible for imparting knowledge, fostering critical thinking, and nurturing the growth of students. However, in order to effectively fulfill these responsibilities, teachers need to be equipped with the necessary skills, knowledge, and ongoing professional development.

Teacher training and professional development are essential components of any successful education system. They ensure that educators stay updated with the latest pedagogical approaches, instructional strategies, and subject knowledge, enabling them to provide high-quality education to their students. This subchapter aims to provide valuable insights into the importance of teacher training and professional development in comparative and international education.

One of the key aspects of teacher training is the acquisition of subject-specific knowledge. Teachers need to have a deep understanding of the subjects they teach to effectively communicate concepts and foster a love for learning in their students. Additionally, they must be aware of the latest educational practices and methodologies that can enhance their teaching effectiveness.

Furthermore, teacher training programs should also focus on developing pedagogical skills. These skills include lesson planning, classroom management, assessment strategies, and effective communication techniques. By honing these skills, teachers can create a conducive learning environment and cater to the diverse needs of their students.

In addition to initial teacher training, ongoing professional development is crucial for teachers to stay abreast of advancements in education. Professional development programs provide teachers with opportunities to engage in workshops, seminars, and conferences that enhance their teaching practices. They can learn from experts in the field, collaborate with other educators, and share best practices.

Moreover, teacher training and professional development should also address the issue of diversity in the classroom. In today's globalized world, classrooms are becoming increasingly diverse, with students from various cultural, linguistic, and socio-economic backgrounds. Teachers need to be equipped with culturally responsive teaching strategies and intercultural competence to effectively engage and support all students.

In conclusion, teacher training and professional development are integral to the success of any education system. By investing in the continuous development of teachers, we ensure that they are equipped with the necessary skills, knowledge, and tools to provide high-quality education to students. Furthermore, addressing the issue of diversity in teacher training and professional development programs is essential to create inclusive learning environments. Comparative and international education research plays a vital role in identifying best practices and facilitating the exchange of knowledge and experiences across different education systems.

Education Systems in Japan

Japan is renowned for its highly successful education system, which consistently ranks among the top in international assessments such as the Programme for International Student Assessment (PISA). This subchapter provides a comprehensive overview of the education systems in Japan, highlighting its unique features and key factors contributing to its success.

The foundation of Japan's education system lies in its commitment to providing equal opportunities for all children to receive quality education. The system is divided into three levels: elementary, lower secondary, and upper secondary education. Compulsory education is mandated for children aged 6 to 15, ensuring that every child has access to basic education.

At the elementary level, students receive a broad education that focuses on developing fundamental skills in subjects such as math, science, language, and social studies. The curriculum emphasizes both academic knowledge and character development, fostering a sense of discipline, responsibility, and respect for others.

Lower secondary education builds upon the elementary curriculum, with a greater emphasis on academic subjects. Students explore a wide range of subjects, including Japanese language, mathematics, science, social studies, music, and physical education. Additionally, they are encouraged to participate in club activities, which promote teamwork and develop various skills and interests.

Upper secondary education in Japan is not compulsory, but the majority of students choose to continue their education at this level. This stage is characterized by a more specialized and rigorous curriculum. Students can select from two paths: academic or vocational. The academic track prepares students for university entrance examinations, while the vocational track focuses on developing practical skills for specific careers.

One key aspect of Japan's education system is the strong emphasis on teacher professionalism and commitment to continuous professional development. Teachers are highly respected and play a crucial role in shaping students' academic and personal development. They undergo rigorous training and are provided with ongoing support and opportunities for professional growth.

Another contributing factor to Japan's educational success is the importance placed on parental involvement. Parents are actively engaged in their children's education, attending parent-teacher meetings and collaborating with teachers to support their children's learning.

In conclusion, Japan's education system is characterized by its commitment to equal opportunities, emphasis on academic and character development, highly trained teachers, and strong parental involvement. These factors have contributed to the system's consistent success and high rankings in international assessments. By understanding the unique features of Japan's education system, educators and policymakers can gain valuable insights into effective practices that promote academic excellence and holistic development for students worldwide.

Structure and Organization

In the realm of comparative and international education, understanding the diverse structures and organizations of education systems is crucial. In this subchapter, we delve into the intricate details of how education systems are structured and organized across the globe. This knowledge is essential for educators, policymakers, researchers, and anyone interested in gaining a comprehensive understanding of global education systems.

Firstly, we explore the different models of education systems found worldwide. From the highly centralized systems to those with greater decentralization, each model has its own strengths and weaknesses. We examine the advantages and disadvantages of centralized systems, where decision-making power is primarily held at the national level, versus decentralized systems, which involve greater local autonomy. By comparing and contrasting these models, we can gain insights into their impact on educational outcomes and the factors contributing to their success or failure.

Next, we delve into the organizational structures within education systems. We analyze the roles and responsibilities of key stakeholders, such as government bodies, educational institutions, teachers, students, parents, and communities. Understanding these roles is crucial for fostering effective collaboration and ensuring the smooth functioning of education systems. We also explore the different levels of governance and decision-making processes within education systems, ranging from national to regional and local levels. This examination provides valuable insights into how policies are formulated and implemented, and how educational resources are allocated.

Furthermore, we investigate the influence of cultural, social, and economic factors on the structure and organization of education systems. By examining case studies from various countries, we highlight the ways in which cultural values, social norms, and economic conditions shape education policies, curriculum development, and teaching practices. This understanding helps us appreciate the diversity and uniqueness of education systems globally, as well as the challenges and opportunities they face.

Lastly, we discuss the role of comparative and international education in shaping and improving education systems. By studying successful practices and innovative approaches from different countries, we can identify strategies that can be adapted and implemented elsewhere. We emphasize the importance of cross-cultural understanding, knowledge exchange, and collaboration among countries to foster continuous improvement and enhance the quality of education worldwide.

In conclusion, this subchapter on "Structure and Organization" provides a comprehensive overview of the diverse education systems found globally. It offers valuable insights for a wide range of audiences, including educators, policymakers, researchers, and anyone interested in comparative and international education. By understanding the various models, organizational structures, and influences on education systems, we can work towards creating more effective, inclusive, and equitable educational opportunities for all.

Curriculum and Assessment

In the ever-evolving landscape of education, the design and implementation of curriculum and assessment play a pivotal role in shaping the learning experiences of students worldwide. This subchapter delves into the significance of these two key components in the realm of comparative and international education.

The curriculum serves as the backbone of any educational system, acting as a blueprint for what students will learn and the skills they will acquire. However, it is important to acknowledge the inherent diversity that exists across global education systems. While some countries prioritize a standardized curriculum, others embrace a more flexible approach that allows for regional or local variations. Understanding these differences is crucial for educators, policymakers, and researchers involved in comparative and international education.

By examining various curriculum models from around the world, we can gain valuable insights into how different societies prioritize certain knowledge, skills, and values. This exploration enables us to appreciate the unique cultural, social, and economic contexts that shape educational goals and expectations. Furthermore, it highlights the need for a balanced curriculum that encompasses both universal knowledge and local relevance.

Assessment, on the other hand, plays a vital role in measuring students' progress and ensuring that curriculum goals are being met. However, the methods and approaches to assessment can vary significantly across different education systems. Some countries rely heavily on standardized tests, while others emphasize project-based assignments, portfolios, or teacher evaluations.

This subchapter will examine the advantages and disadvantages of various assessment methods and their impact on students' learning experiences. It will shed light on the potential biases and limitations of standardized tests, as well as the potential benefits of more holistic and authentic forms of assessment. By comparing different assessment practices, we can cultivate a deeper understanding of how they influence teaching and learning, and ultimately, student success.

Moreover, this subchapter will explore the ongoing debate regarding the role of assessment in fostering creativity, critical thinking, and problem-solving skills. In an era where the demands of the workforce are rapidly evolving, it is crucial to reevaluate assessment practices to ensure they align with the needs of the 21st-century learner.

In conclusion, this subchapter on Curriculum and Assessment provides a comprehensive exploration of these fundamental aspects of education. By understanding the diversity of curriculum models and assessment practices across global education systems, we can gain valuable insights into how different societies approach teaching and learning. This knowledge is essential for educators, policymakers, and researchers engaged in comparative and international education, as it allows us to identify best practices, foster innovation, and promote educational equity and excellence for all.

Teacher Training and Professional Development

In today's globalized world, education plays a vital role in shaping the future of nations. As societies become increasingly diverse, it is crucial to equip teachers with the necessary skills and knowledge to effectively address the needs of a diverse student population. This subchapter explores the importance of teacher training and professional development in the context of comparative and international education.

Teacher training programs are designed to prepare educators for the challenges they may encounter in the classroom. These programs focus on developing pedagogical skills, content knowledge, and cultural competence. Pedagogical skills encompass various teaching strategies, classroom management techniques, and assessment methods that enable teachers to create inclusive and engaging learning environments. Content knowledge refers to deep understanding of the subjects they teach, enabling teachers to deliver accurate and relevant information. Cultural competence is a critical aspect of teacher training, as it equips educators with the ability to understand and appreciate diverse cultural backgrounds, languages, and learning styles of their students.

Professional development is an ongoing process that enables teachers to continually update their knowledge and skills throughout their careers. It provides opportunities for teachers to engage in reflection, collaborate with colleagues, and explore innovative teaching practices. Professional development programs can take various forms, such as workshops, conferences, online courses, and mentoring programs. These initiatives allow teachers to stay informed about the latest research and best practices in education, ultimately enhancing their effectiveness in the classroom.

In comparative and international education, teacher training and professional development take on added significance. As educators work with students from different cultural, linguistic, and socioeconomic backgrounds, they must be equipped with the tools to navigate these complexities. By comparing education systems from around the world, educators can gain insights into effective strategies for teaching diverse student populations. They can learn from the experiences of other countries and adapt successful practices to their own classrooms.

In conclusion, teacher training and professional development play a vital role in preparing educators to meet the diverse needs of students in a globalized world. By acquiring pedagogical skills, content knowledge, and cultural competence, teachers can create inclusive and engaging learning environments. Ongoing professional development ensures that educators stay abreast of the latest research and best practices in education. In the field of comparative and international education, teacher training and professional development offer valuable insights into effective strategies for teaching diverse student populations. Ultimately, investing in the training and development of teachers is paramount to fostering inclusive and quality education systems worldwide.

Chapter 7: Education Systems in Africa

Overview of Education Systems in South Africa

South Africa, a diverse and vibrant country located in the southernmost part of the African continent, is renowned for its rich cultural heritage and powerful historical background. In recent years, the nation has made significant progress in its education sector, aiming to provide equal opportunities for all citizens to access quality education. This chapter will provide an overview of the education systems in South Africa, highlighting key aspects and challenges faced in the pursuit of achieving educational excellence.

The education system in South Africa is divided into three levels: primary education, secondary education, and tertiary education. Primary education, which starts at the age of six, consists of seven years of compulsory education. This phase focuses on developing basic literacy and numeracy skills, as well as nurturing social and emotional growth. Secondary education, spanning five years, is divided into lower secondary and upper secondary levels. Students at this stage can choose between academic or vocational pathways, based on their interests and career aspirations.

Despite efforts to improve educational outcomes, South Africa faces numerous challenges. One of the primary concerns is the persistent inequality in access to quality education. Historically, apartheid policies created stark disparities in education, resulting in segregated schools that catered to specific racial groups. Although significant progress has been made in dismantling these inequalities, the legacy of apartheid still lingers, particularly in underprivileged communities.

The education system also grapples with issues such as overcrowded classrooms, a shortage of qualified teachers, and a lack of resources. These challenges often hinder effective teaching and learning, leading to low academic performance and limited opportunities for students to reach their full potential. Additionally, the country faces high dropout rates, especially in secondary education, which exacerbates the issue of youth unemployment.

To address these challenges, the South African government has implemented various initiatives. These include the introduction of interventions to improve teacher training and support, the expansion of early childhood development programs, and the establishment of special schools to cater to students with disabilities. Efforts have also been made to increase access to technology and digital resources in schools, facilitating a more inclusive and technologically advanced learning environment.

In conclusion, South Africa's education system has undergone significant transformation to ensure that all citizens have access to quality education. While progress has been made, there are still challenges to overcome. By addressing issues of inequality, improving infrastructure and resources, and investing in teacher development, South Africa can continue its journey towards an inclusive and equitable education system that empowers all learners to thrive.

Structure and Organization

In the realm of education, structure and organization play a crucial role in shaping the success and effectiveness of any education system. This subchapter explores the various aspects of structure and organization within global education systems, providing comparative insights and highlighting the importance of understanding diversity in this context.

The structure of an education system refers to the overall framework and arrangement of its components. It encompasses the hierarchy and relationships between different levels of education, such as primary, secondary, and tertiary education. Comparative analysis of education systems around the world reveals intriguing variations in their structures, reflecting diverse cultural, social, and historical contexts.

One key aspect of structure is the organization and management of educational institutions. This includes the allocation of resources, decision-making processes, and the roles and responsibilities of educational stakeholders. By examining how different countries and regions organize their education systems, we gain valuable insights into their priorities, values, and approaches to education.

Understanding the diversity in global education systems is essential for comparative and international education scholars. By exploring the structures and organizations of different systems, researchers can identify effective practices and policies that can be adapted to improve educational outcomes in their own contexts. This subchapter aims to equip scholars and practitioners with the knowledge and tools to navigate this complex landscape.

Moreover, this subchapter acknowledges the importance of context and local factors in shaping the structure and organization of education systems. It delves into case studies from various countries, shedding light on how historical, political, and cultural factors influence the design and implementation of education policies. By examining these cases, readers will gain a deeper understanding of the unique challenges and opportunities that arise in different educational contexts.

In conclusion, the subchapter on Structure and Organization provides a comprehensive exploration of the diverse education systems around the world. It emphasizes the significance of understanding the various structures and organizations within these systems, as well as the importance of comparative analysis in identifying effective practices. This subchapter is a valuable resource for scholars and practitioners in the field of comparative and international education, offering insights and knowledge that can contribute to the improvement of education worldwide.

Curriculum and Assessment

In the realm of education, curriculum and assessment play crucial roles in shaping the learning experiences of students and determining their academic progress. The design and implementation of curriculum and assessment methods vary significantly across different countries and education systems. Understanding the diversity in curriculum and assessment approaches is essential for educators, policymakers, and researchers in the field of comparative and international education.

Curriculum refers to the content, skills, and knowledge that students are expected to learn within a specific educational program. It encompasses not only subject-specific material but also the development of critical thinking, problem-solving skills, and social and emotional competencies. While some countries adhere to a standardized national curriculum, others provide more flexibility at the regional or local level. The subchapter on curriculum will explore the strengths and weaknesses of these approaches, considering factors such as cultural relevance, student engagement, and the balance between breadth and depth of knowledge.

Assessment, on the other hand, refers to the methods used to evaluate student learning and achievement. It can take various forms, including tests, exams, projects, portfolios, and performance-based assessments. The subchapter on assessment will delve into the different approaches employed in various education systems, examining their effectiveness in measuring student progress and informing instructional practices. The chapter will also explore the debate surrounding standardized testing and alternative assessment methods, highlighting their impact on student motivation, equity, and overall educational outcomes.

By examining curriculum and assessment practices from a comparative perspective, this subchapter aims to provide insights into the strengths and weaknesses of different education systems worldwide. It will highlight the importance of considering context-specific factors, such as cultural values, educational goals, and socioeconomic conditions, when designing and implementing curriculum and assessment strategies. Moreover, it will emphasize the need for ongoing research, collaboration, and knowledge-sharing among educators and policymakers to foster continuous improvement and innovation in education.

This subchapter is a valuable resource for educators, policymakers, and researchers in the field of comparative and international education. By understanding the diversity in curriculum and assessment approaches across the globe, readers will gain a deeper appreciation for the different educational philosophies and practices that shape students' learning experiences. Ultimately, the goal is to foster an inclusive and equitable educational landscape that prepares students to thrive in an increasingly interconnected and diverse world.

Teacher Training and Professional Development

In the ever-changing landscape of education, it is crucial for teachers to continuously adapt and grow in order to meet the diverse needs of their students. Teacher training and professional development play a significant role in equipping educators with the necessary skills and knowledge to excel in their profession. This subchapter will delve into the importance of teacher training and professional development in the context of comparative and international education.

Teacher training programs serve as the foundation for preparing individuals to enter the teaching profession. These programs provide aspiring teachers with a comprehensive understanding of pedagogy, subject matter knowledge, and classroom management techniques. By focusing on the development of effective teaching strategies, these programs ensure that teachers are equipped to create inclusive and engaging learning environments for their students.

Beyond initial teacher training, ongoing professional development is essential for educators to stay up-to-date with the latest research, best practices, and technological advancements. Professional development opportunities allow teachers to enhance their teaching skills, explore innovative teaching methods, and collaborate with their peers. By participating in workshops, conferences, and online courses, teachers can continuously expand their knowledge base and refine their instructional practices.

In the field of comparative and international education, teacher training and professional development take on an added dimension. As educators work with an increasingly diverse student population, it is crucial for them to be aware of cultural differences, linguistic variations, and varying learning styles. Teacher training programs and professional development initiatives should therefore incorporate modules that highlight the importance of cultural competence and inclusive teaching practices.

Moreover, comparative and international education emphasizes the importance of understanding different education systems, policies, and practices from around the world. Teacher training programs should expose educators to these global perspectives, enabling them to incorporate international elements into their teaching. Professional development opportunities can further enhance this global perspective by facilitating collaborations and knowledge sharing between educators from different countries.

In conclusion, teacher training and professional development are vital components of the education system, particularly in the realm of comparative and international education. By continuously honing their skills and staying abreast of global trends, teachers can provide students with a high-quality education that prepares them for an interconnected world. Whether you are an educator, policymaker, or education enthusiast, understanding the significance of teacher training and professional development is essential for promoting excellence in education and fostering inclusive learning environments.

Education Systems in Nigeria

Education is a fundamental human right that plays a crucial role in shaping individuals and societies. Understanding the diversity of education systems across the globe is essential to gain insights into various approaches and challenges faced by different countries. In this subchapter, we will delve into the education system in Nigeria, a country with a rich cultural heritage and a rapidly growing population.

Nigeria, located in West Africa, is the most populous country on the African continent. With over 200 million people and a diverse range of ethnic groups, Nigeria's education system is a complex and multifaceted one. The system is divided into different levels, including pre-primary, primary, secondary, and tertiary education.

At the pre-primary level, children aged three to five can attend early childhood education centers, although access to these centers remains limited, particularly in rural areas. Primary education is compulsory and lasts for six years, starting at age six. The curriculum focuses on core subjects such as Mathematics, English, Social Studies, and Basic Science.

Secondary education in Nigeria is divided into junior and senior secondary levels. Junior secondary education lasts for three years, while senior secondary education lasts for another three years. At the end of senior secondary education, students sit for the West African Senior School Certificate Examination (WASSCE), which is a crucial examination for further education and employment opportunities.

Tertiary education in Nigeria is provided by universities, polytechnics, and colleges of education. Universities offer undergraduate and postgraduate programs, while polytechnics and colleges of education focus on technical and vocational training. Nigerian universities have gained recognition globally, attracting students from various countries.

Despite the significant progress made in the Nigerian education system, it faces several challenges. These challenges include inadequate funding, insufficient infrastructure, low teacher quality, and high dropout rates. Additionally, there are significant regional disparities in access to quality education, with urban areas having better educational facilities compared to rural areas.

Understanding the diversity of education systems in Nigeria is crucial for comparative and international education practitioners and researchers. By examining the Nigerian education system, we can gain insights into the challenges faced by a rapidly growing population with diverse cultural backgrounds. This knowledge can help inform policies and interventions to improve education access, quality, and outcomes not only in Nigeria but also in other countries facing similar issues.

In conclusion, the education system in Nigeria is a complex and diverse one, reflecting the country's rich cultural heritage and large population. By exploring the challenges and successes of the Nigerian education system, we can gain valuable insights into the broader field of comparative and international education.

Structure and Organization

In order to fully understand the complexities and nuances of global education systems, it is essential to delve into the structure and organization that underpin them. The way educational institutions are structured and organized can greatly influence the quality and accessibility of education, as well as the opportunities available to students. This subchapter aims to provide insights into the various structures and organizational models found in education systems across the globe, with a focus on comparative and international perspectives.

One of the key aspects of structure and organization in education is the division of educational levels. In many countries, education is divided into primary, secondary, and tertiary levels. However, the specific age ranges and curriculum content can vary significantly from one country to another. Understanding these differences is crucial for policymakers and educators to create effective policies and curricula that meet the needs of students at each educational level.

Another important aspect of structure and organization in education is the governance and administration of educational institutions. This includes the roles and responsibilities of various stakeholders, such as government bodies, school boards, and principals. Comparative insights into different governance models can shed light on the strengths and weaknesses of different approaches, helping policymakers and educators make informed decisions about educational administration and management.

Furthermore, the subchapter will explore the organizational structures within schools themselves. This includes examining various models of classroom organization, such as traditional lecture-style classrooms versus more student-centered approaches. Additionally, the subchapter will delve into the organizational structures within schools, such as departmentalization or grade-level team teaching, and their impact on student learning outcomes.

A comparative and international perspective is vital in understanding diversity in education systems. By examining different structures and organizational models across countries, we can identify best practices and innovative approaches that can be adapted and implemented in different contexts. Additionally, understanding the challenges and limitations of different structures can help policymakers and educators avoid potential pitfalls and develop more effective strategies for educational improvement.

In conclusion, the structure and organization of education systems play a crucial role in shaping the quality and accessibility of education. This subchapter provides a comprehensive exploration of the various structures and organizational models found in education systems globally. By examining and comparing these models, we can gain valuable insights into how to improve education and ensure equitable opportunities for all students. Whether you are a policy maker, educator, or simply interested in comparative and international education, this subchapter will deepen your understanding of the complexities and possibilities within global education systems.

Curriculum and Assessment

In the realm of education, curriculum and assessment are two crucial components that shape the learning experience of students. Understanding the diversity of global education systems requires a keen examination of how different countries approach curriculum development and assessment practices. This subchapter delves into the complex interplay between curriculum and assessment, shedding light on the comparative insights that can be gained from studying these aspects.

Curriculum refers to the planned and organized set of knowledge, skills, and competencies that students are expected to acquire during their educational journey. It encompasses not only subject-specific content but also the development of critical thinking, problem-solving abilities, and socio-emotional skills. Comparative and international education scholars recognize that curricula vary significantly across countries, influenced by cultural, historical, and socio-economic factors.

One aspect worth exploring is the extent of standardization or flexibility within curricula. Some education systems favor a centralized approach, where a national curriculum framework is followed uniformly across all schools. Others prioritize local autonomy, allowing individual schools or regions to adapt the curriculum to meet their specific needs. Understanding these different approaches can provide valuable insights into the strengths and weaknesses of various systems.

Assessment, on the other hand, refers to the methods used to evaluate student learning and progress. It plays a crucial role in measuring the effectiveness of the curriculum and informing instructional practices.

Comparative and international education researchers examine the diversity of assessment practices, ranging from high-stakes examinations to project-based assessments and portfolios.

Exploring the relationship between curriculum and assessment is essential to ensure that educational goals are aligned with the evaluation methods employed. A curriculum that emphasizes critical thinking and problem-solving skills, for example, may require a more holistic assessment approach, rather than relying solely on standardized tests. By comparing how different education systems strike this balance, scholars and practitioners can gain valuable insights into best practices and potential areas for improvement.

Overall, this subchapter aims to provide a comprehensive understanding of how curriculum and assessment shape global education systems. By examining the diverse approaches taken by various countries, scholars and educators can gain valuable insights into the strengths and weaknesses of different systems. This knowledge is crucial for fostering an inclusive and effective education that meets the needs of all learners, regardless of their cultural or socio-economic backgrounds.

Teacher Training and Professional Development

In today's diverse and rapidly changing world, the role of teachers has become increasingly crucial in shaping the education system and ensuring inclusive learning environments for all students. Teacher training and professional development play a pivotal role in equipping educators with the necessary skills, knowledge, and attitudes to meet the diverse needs of their students and effectively navigate the complexities of the education system. This subchapter delves into the importance of teacher training and professional development in the context of comparative and international education.

Teacher training programs are designed to provide aspiring educators with the foundational knowledge and pedagogical skills required to become effective teachers. These programs typically include coursework in educational theory, child development, curriculum design, and classroom management. Additionally, teacher training programs should incorporate modules on diversity, equity, and inclusion, as these concepts are essential for fostering inclusive learning environments.

Professional development, on the other hand, refers to continuous learning opportunities that educators engage in throughout their careers to enhance their teaching practices and stay abreast of research and emerging trends in education. Often facilitated through workshops, conferences, and online courses, professional development enables teachers to refine their instructional strategies, integrate technology into their classrooms, and deepen their understanding of diverse student populations.

Comparative and international education recognizes the importance of teacher training and professional development in improving the quality of education systems worldwide. It encourages cross-country collaboration and knowledge sharing, allowing educators to learn from each other's experiences and best practices. By examining different educational systems and approaches, educators can gain new perspectives and insights that can inform their own teaching practices.

Moreover, teacher training and professional development must be tailored to address the unique challenges and needs of specific contexts. For instance, in countries with large immigrant populations, training programs should focus on equipping educators with the skills to support English language learners and promote cultural competency. In regions affected by conflict or poverty, professional development should emphasize trauma-informed teaching strategies and community engagement.

In conclusion, teacher training and professional development are integral components of comparative and international education. By investing in the continuous growth and development of educators, we can ensure that they are well-equipped to meet the diverse needs of their students and drive positive change within education systems worldwide. Through collaboration, knowledge sharing, and a commitment to inclusivity, we can create a future where every student has access to a quality education, regardless of their background or circumstances.

Chapter 8: Education Systems in Oceania

Overview of Education Systems in Australia

Australia is renowned for its high-quality education system, which is known for its strong focus on innovation, diversity, and inclusivity. As one of the leading countries in the field of education, Australia offers a wide range of opportunities for students of all ages and backgrounds.

The education system in Australia is divided into three main levels: primary education, secondary education, and tertiary education. Primary education typically begins at the age of five or six and lasts for six years, while secondary education spans from Year 7 to Year 12. Tertiary education includes universities, vocational education, and training institutions.

One of the key strengths of the Australian education system is its emphasis on equality and inclusivity. The government strives to provide equal opportunities for all students, regardless of their socio-economic background or geographic location. This commitment is reflected in the provision of free public education for all Australian citizens and permanent residents.

In terms of curriculum, each state and territory in Australia has its own education system, resulting in some variations across the country. However, there is a strong focus on core subjects such as English, mathematics, science, and humanities, complemented by a range of elective subjects that allow students to explore their individual interests and talents.

Another notable aspect of the Australian education system is its emphasis on vocational education and training (VET). VET courses provide students with practical skills and knowledge that are directly applicable to the workforce. These courses are offered at both secondary and tertiary levels and are highly valued by employers.

Australia is also home to several world-class universities that attract international students from all over the globe. The country's higher education sector offers a wide range of courses and degrees, ranging from undergraduate to postgraduate levels. Australian universities are known for their research-intensive approach and commitment to producing graduates who are well-equipped for the global job market.

In conclusion, the education system in Australia is highly regarded for its commitment to inclusivity, diversity, and innovation. With a strong focus on providing equal opportunities for all students, Australia offers a range of educational pathways to suit individual needs and interests. From primary to tertiary education, students in Australia have access to high-quality education that equips them with the skills and knowledge needed for success in the globalized world.

Structure and Organization

In the world of education systems, understanding the structure and organization of different models is crucial. This subchapter delves into the intricate details of how education systems are designed and managed globally, providing comparative insights into various approaches.

At the heart of any education system lies its structure, which encompasses the overall framework and organization of schools, curricula, and policies. A comparative analysis of education systems around the world allows us to examine the similarities and differences in their structure and organization, providing valuable insights for educators, policymakers, and researchers.

One key aspect of structure and organization is the governance and administration of education systems. Different countries adopt various models, including centralized, decentralized, or hybrid systems. This subchapter explores the advantages and challenges associated with each approach, shedding light on how decisions are made, resources are allocated, and accountability is ensured.

Another crucial element is the curriculum and instructional design. Education systems worldwide differ in terms of the subjects offered, pedagogical approaches, and assessment methods. By examining the structure and organization of curricula, we can identify the underlying philosophies, priorities, and cultural influences that shape the education systems of different countries.

Furthermore, this subchapter addresses the role of teachers and their professional development within education systems. It examines the qualifications, training, and ongoing support provided to teachers globally, highlighting the impact on instructional quality and student outcomes. Understanding the diverse approaches to teacher education and professional development can inform policies and practices aimed at improving teaching and learning worldwide.

Lastly, the subchapter explores the role of technology and digital resources in education systems. With the rapid advancement of technology, its integration into education has become a global phenomenon. Understanding how different education systems incorporate technology and leverage digital resources can provide insights into effective implementation strategies, challenges, and potential benefits.

Overall, this subchapter on Structure and Organization provides a comprehensive overview of the diverse approaches to education systems worldwide. By examining governance and administration, curriculum design, teacher training, and technology integration, it equips readers with valuable knowledge to enhance their understanding of comparative and international education. Whether you are an educator, policymaker, or researcher, this subchapter offers a wealth of insights into the complexities of education systems and their impact on diverse populations.

Curriculum and Assessment

In the realm of education, the design and implementation of a comprehensive curriculum and effective assessment strategies are crucial components for achieving successful learning outcomes. The subchapter on "Curriculum and Assessment" in the book "Understanding Diversity: Comparative Insights into Global Education Systems" offers valuable insights into the various approaches adopted by different countries in the field of comparative and international education.

The subchapter begins by exploring the concept of curriculum, emphasizing its role as a framework that guides the teaching and learning process. Recognizing the importance of accommodating diverse student populations, the chapter delves into how different countries develop their curricula to address the needs, interests, and abilities of their students. By comparing and contrasting these approaches, readers gain a deeper understanding of the role of curriculum in shaping educational experiences.

Assessment is another significant aspect of the subchapter, as it provides a means to measure student progress and achievement. The book offers an in-depth analysis of the diverse assessment practices across various global education systems. It explores the different assessment tools and techniques used, ranging from traditional examinations to project-based assessments and portfolios. By examining the strengths and weaknesses of each approach, the subchapter highlights the importance of aligning assessment strategies with the goals and objectives of the curriculum.

Furthermore, the subchapter addresses the challenges faced by educators in implementing effective curriculum and assessment practices. These challenges include striking a balance between local and global perspectives, ensuring cultural relevance, and promoting inclusivity. Through real-life examples and case studies, the chapter demonstrates how countries have tackled these challenges, providing readers with valuable insights and potential solutions.

The subchapter concludes by discussing the impact of curriculum and assessment on student learning outcomes and educational equity. It highlights the importance of a well-designed curriculum that caters to the needs of all students, regardless of their cultural, linguistic, or socioeconomic backgrounds. Additionally, it emphasizes the significance of fair and inclusive assessment practices in promoting educational equity and ensuring that all students have an equal opportunity to succeed.

"Curriculum and Assessment" is a subchapter that appeals to a wide audience, ranging from educators and policymakers to researchers and students interested in comparative and international education. By examining the approaches taken by various countries, this subchapter provides a comprehensive understanding of the complexities involved in designing and implementing effective curriculum and assessment practices. It encourages readers to critically analyze their own education systems, identify areas for improvement, and ultimately work towards creating more inclusive and equitable learning environments for all students.

Teacher Training and Professional Development

In today's rapidly changing and diverse world, the role of teachers has become more crucial than ever. They are not only responsible for imparting knowledge but also for shaping the minds of future generations. Therefore, it is essential to ensure that teachers are equipped with the necessary skills and knowledge to meet the diverse needs of their students. This subchapter explores the significance of teacher training and professional development in the context of comparative and international education.

Teacher training programs play a vital role in preparing educators to tackle the challenges posed by diverse student populations. These programs focus on developing pedagogical techniques, cultural competence, and inclusive teaching strategies. By providing teachers with a comprehensive understanding of diverse cultures, languages, and learning styles, training programs empower them to create inclusive and equitable learning environments.

Professional development is an ongoing process that enables teachers to continuously update their skills and knowledge. It encourages teachers to engage in reflective practice and encourages collaboration among educators. Professional development opportunities can take various forms, such as workshops, conferences, online courses, and peer mentoring programs. These opportunities allow teachers to share best practices, learn from one another, and stay up-to-date with the latest research and educational trends.

In the field of comparative and international education, teacher training and professional development have gained significant attention. As education systems become more globalized, teachers are increasingly interacting with students from diverse cultural and linguistic backgrounds. This necessitates a deep understanding of different educational systems and teaching practices. Comparative education provides valuable insights into various educational models, allowing teachers to adapt and implement effective strategies in their own classrooms.

Furthermore, teacher training and professional development contribute to the overall improvement of education systems. Well-trained and competent teachers have a positive impact on student achievement, school climate, and community engagement. By investing in teacher training and professional development, countries can enhance the quality of education and promote social cohesion.

In conclusion, teacher training and professional development are crucial components of a successful education system. By equipping teachers with the necessary skills and knowledge, we can ensure that all students receive a high-quality education. Comparative and international education provide valuable insights into diverse educational systems, fostering a global perspective among educators. Ultimately, investing in teacher training and professional development is an investment in the future of education and the well-being of our global society.

Education Systems in New Zealand

Education is a fundamental aspect of any society, shaping the minds and futures of individuals. In the global context, it is crucial to understand the diversity that exists in education systems worldwide. One such system worth exploring is the education system in New Zealand. This subchapter delves into the key aspects of the New Zealand education system, offering comparative insights for a diverse audience interested in comparative and international education.

New Zealand takes pride in its comprehensive and inclusive education system, designed to cater to the needs of every student. The system is based on the principles of equity, access, and excellence. Education in New Zealand is compulsory for children aged 6 to 16, with most students attending state-funded schools. However, the country also boasts a significant number of private schools, known as independent schools, which offer alternative educational approaches.

One notable feature of the New Zealand education system is its commitment to the Treaty of Waitangi, an agreement between the indigenous Māori people and the British Crown. The treaty provides a framework for cultural partnership, making Māori language and culture an integral part of the curriculum. This emphasis on biculturalism sets the New Zealand education system apart from many others globally.

Another distinctive aspect of the New Zealand education system is its focus on holistic development. The curriculum, known as Te Whāriki, emphasizes not only academic learning but also social, emotional, and physical development. The aim is to produce well-rounded individuals who are equipped for life beyond the classroom.

The New Zealand education system also promotes student-centered learning, encouraging critical thinking, problem-solving, and creativity. Teachers act as facilitators, guiding students in their learning journey rather than just transmitting knowledge. This approach fosters independent thinking and prepares students for an ever-changing world.

Additionally, New Zealand places great importance on early childhood education. The government provides subsidies to ensure that all children have access to quality early learning experiences. This commitment has led to high enrollment rates and improved school readiness for children entering primary education.

In conclusion, the New Zealand education system offers valuable insights into the diversity and inclusiveness that can be achieved in comparative and international education. Its commitment to equity, biculturalism, holistic development, and student-centered learning sets it apart. By understanding the New Zealand education system, we can learn from its successes and adapt its principles to our own educational contexts, ultimately striving for more inclusive and effective education systems worldwide.

Structure and Organization

In the realm of education systems, structure and organization play a pivotal role in shaping the learning experiences of students. This subchapter explores the various aspects of structure and organization within global education systems, providing comparative insights into their significance and impact.

One of the key aspects to consider is the organizational structure of educational institutions. While there may be variations across countries, the fundamental objective remains the same – to provide a conducive environment for learning. This subchapter delves into the different models of organizational structures, such as centralized, decentralized, and hybrid systems, and examines how they impact the overall functioning of educational institutions.

Furthermore, the subchapter explores the role of governance in education systems. Different countries adopt distinct governance models, ranging from centralized government control to decentralized decision-making processes. Understanding the relationship between governance and educational outcomes is crucial for policymakers and education practitioners alike. By analyzing the strengths and weaknesses of various governance models, this subchapter aims to provide valuable insights into the impact of governance on educational quality and equity.

Additionally, the subchapter sheds light on the organizational practices within education systems. It delves into topics such as curriculum development, assessment methods, and teacher training programs. By comparing these practices across different countries, readers gain a deeper understanding of the factors that contribute to successful educational outcomes. Furthermore, this exploration helps identify innovative practices that can be adapted and implemented in diverse contexts.

Moreover, the subchapter discusses the role of technology in shaping the structure and organization of education systems. With the increasing integration of technology in classrooms, it is essential to examine how it influences teaching methods, student engagement, and administrative processes. By examining the experiences of various countries, readers gain insights into the potential benefits and challenges associated with the use of technology in education.

Overall, this subchapter on structure and organization provides an invaluable resource for those interested in comparative and international education. By exploring the various aspects of structure and organization, readers gain a comprehensive understanding of the factors that shape education systems worldwide. Whether you are a policymaker, researcher, or educator, the insights presented in this subchapter will help you navigate the complexities of global education systems and contribute to the enhancement of educational quality and equity on an international scale.

Curriculum and Assessment

Curriculum and Assessment: Shaping Global Education Systems

In the increasingly interconnected and diverse world we live in, education plays a vital role in preparing individuals to thrive in a global society. As we strive to understand and embrace diversity, it is essential to examine the curriculum and assessment methods employed in different education systems across the globe. This subchapter aims to shed light on the significance of curriculum and assessment in fostering inclusive and effective learning environments, with a focus on comparative and international education.

Curriculum, the foundation of any education system, encompasses the knowledge, skills, and values that educators aim to impart to their students. It serves as a roadmap, guiding both teachers and learners through the educational journey. However, the content and structure of curricula vary greatly from one country to another, reflecting the unique cultural, political, and social contexts in which they operate.

Understanding and comparing different curricula can provide valuable insights into how education systems address diversity and promote inclusivity. By examining the ways in which various cultures and societies approach education, we can identify commonalities, challenges, and effective practices that can be adapted and implemented across borders.

Assessment is another critical aspect of education that warrants examination. It not only measures students' understanding and progress but also shapes teaching practices and educational policies. However, assessment methods can be culturally biased, favoring certain groups and marginalizing others. Hence, it is crucial to explore alternative assessment strategies that promote equity and inclusivity.

This subchapter will delve into the diverse approaches to curriculum development and assessment methods in different countries, highlighting the strengths and weaknesses of each system. By studying the successes and failures of these approaches, educators, policymakers, and researchers can gain valuable insights into how to foster inclusive learning environments that cater to the needs of all learners, irrespective of their cultural, linguistic, or socioeconomic backgrounds.

Moreover, this subchapter will explore the impact of globalization on curriculum and assessment practices. As the world becomes more interconnected, the need for global competencies such as intercultural understanding, critical thinking, and collaboration becomes increasingly important. By examining how education systems around the world integrate these competencies into their curricula and assessments, we can identify best practices and innovative approaches to prepare students for the challenges and opportunities of the 21st century.

In conclusion, the subchapter on Curriculum and Assessment in "Understanding Diversity: Comparative Insights into Global Education Systems" offers a comprehensive exploration of the significance and impact of curriculum and assessment practices in fostering inclusive and effective learning environments. It aims to provide valuable insights to a diverse audience, including educators, policymakers, researchers, and anyone interested in comparative and international education. By studying and understanding the various approaches to curriculum and assessment, we can work towards creating educational systems that celebrate diversity, promote equity, and prepare learners to thrive in an interconnected world.

Teacher Training and Professional Development

In the ever-evolving landscape of education, the role of teachers cannot be overstated. They hold the key to unlocking the potential of students, shaping their minds, and preparing them for the challenges of the future. However, teaching is a complex profession that requires a deep understanding of diverse learners and the ability to adapt to changing educational paradigms. To equip teachers with the necessary skills and knowledge, teacher training and professional development programs play a crucial role in ensuring the quality of education.

Teacher training programs aim to equip educators with the foundational knowledge and skills needed to effectively engage with students from diverse backgrounds. These programs typically cover pedagogical techniques, subject-specific knowledge, classroom management strategies, and assessment methods. However, with the increasing diversity in classrooms, it is essential for these programs to also address cultural competence, inclusivity, and understanding diversity. By fostering an environment of mutual respect and appreciation for differences, teachers can create inclusive classrooms that cater to the needs of all students, regardless of their backgrounds.

Professional development is an ongoing process that helps teachers enhance their skills and stay abreast of current educational trends. It provides opportunities for teachers to engage in reflective practice, collaborate with peers, and explore innovative teaching methodologies. In the realm of comparative and international education, professional development programs take on an added dimension. They enable teachers to gain insights into education systems from around the world, fostering a global perspective that enriches their teaching practices. By exposing teachers to diverse educational contexts, these programs enable them to adapt and incorporate best practices into their own classrooms.

Teacher training and professional development programs should be tailored to meet the specific needs and challenges of each educational system. They should be designed to address the unique cultural, social, and economic factors that shape education in different countries. Additionally, these programs should be accessible to both pre-service and in-service teachers, ensuring that educators at all stages of their careers have opportunities for growth and development.

Understanding the importance of teacher training and professional development is essential for anyone interested in comparative and international education. By investing in the continuous development of teachers, educational systems can create an environment that fosters excellence, inclusivity, and ultimately, prepares students for success in an increasingly interconnected world.

Chapter 9: Key Challenges and Opportunities in Global Education Systems

Access to Education

Education is a fundamental right that should be accessible to every individual, regardless of their background or circumstances. It is the key to unlocking opportunities, empowering individuals, and fostering social and economic development. However, access to education remains a challenge in many parts of the world, highlighting the need for comparative and international perspectives to understand the diversity of global education systems and address these barriers.

In this subchapter, we will explore the issue of access to education, examining the challenges faced by different populations and countries, as well as the strategies and policies implemented to overcome them. By delving into comparative insights, we aim to shed light on the various approaches taken to ensure inclusive and equitable education for all.

One of the primary barriers to access is poverty. In many low-income countries, families struggle to afford the costs associated with education, such as school fees, uniforms, and textbooks. This subchapter will analyze strategies employed by different countries to reduce financial barriers, such as providing free education, scholarships, and stipends for disadvantaged students.

Gender inequality also plays a significant role in limiting access to education. Girls, in particular, face numerous obstacles, including cultural norms, early marriage, and lack of safety. By exploring comparative perspectives, we will uncover successful interventions that have promoted girls' education, such as awareness campaigns, community engagement, and legislative reforms.

Another crucial aspect is the inclusion of marginalized groups, including children with disabilities, refugees, and indigenous populations. By highlighting comparative examples, we will examine how different education systems have strived to create inclusive environments, offering tailored support and resources to ensure equal opportunities for all learners.

Furthermore, this subchapter will address the digital divide, which has become increasingly relevant in the modern era. While technology can enhance access to education, it also creates disparities between those who have access to digital resources and those who do not. We will explore innovative approaches that countries have adopted to bridge this gap, including the provision of digital devices and internet connectivity in remote areas.

In conclusion, access to education is a critical topic within the field of comparative and international education. By examining the challenges, strategies, and policies implemented in diverse global education systems, we can gain valuable insights into improving access for all. This subchapter aims to provide a comprehensive overview of the issue, highlighting best practices and inspiring future endeavors to ensure that education is truly accessible to everyone, regardless of their background or circumstances.

Quality of Education

Education is the cornerstone of societal development and progress. It plays a crucial role in shaping individuals' lives, improving their opportunities, and contributing to the overall well-being of nations. The quality of education, therefore, becomes a fundamental aspect that needs to be carefully examined and evaluated. In this subchapter, we will delve into the concept of quality education and its significance in comparative and international education systems.

Quality education can be defined as the provision of equitable, inclusive, and effective learning experiences that prepare individuals to lead fulfilling lives and contribute to society. It goes beyond mere academic achievement and encompasses a broader set of skills, knowledge, and values necessary for personal growth and active citizenship. In today's globalized world, where the challenges and demands are constantly evolving, the quality of education becomes paramount.

Comparative and international education systems strive to understand the variations in the quality of education across different countries and regions. By examining various indicators such as curriculum, teaching methods, resources, student engagement, and outcomes, researchers and policymakers can identify best practices and areas for improvement. These insights can then be used to inform policy decisions, educational reforms, and international collaborations aimed at enhancing the quality of education worldwide.

One crucial aspect of quality education is equity. Education must be accessible and inclusive, ensuring that all individuals, regardless of their background, have equal opportunities to learn and succeed. This includes addressing disparities in access, retention, and achievement among different socio-economic groups, genders, ethnicities, and abilities. By promoting equity in education, societies can foster social cohesion, reduce inequalities, and empower marginalized communities.

The effectiveness of teaching and learning processes also contributes significantly to the quality of education. Innovative and learner-centered approaches that foster critical thinking, problem-solving, creativity, and collaboration are essential in preparing students for the challenges of the 21st century. Moreover, the availability and adequacy of educational resources, including qualified teachers, well-equipped classrooms, and up-to-date learning materials, are vital factors that influence the quality of education.

In conclusion, the quality of education is a multi-faceted concept that encompasses various dimensions such as equity, effectiveness, and inclusivity. Comparative and international education systems play a pivotal role in understanding and improving the quality of education globally. By examining different factors influencing educational quality and identifying best practices, societies can strive towards providing equitable, inclusive, and effective learning experiences for all individuals. This subchapter aims to shed light on the importance of quality education and its implications for individuals, communities, and nations.

Equity and Inclusion

In today's globalized world, understanding and promoting diversity is crucial for fostering inclusive and equitable education systems. In this subchapter, we delve into the concept of equity and inclusion, examining how different education systems across the globe tackle these issues. By exploring comparative insights, we aim to provide valuable knowledge to a diverse audience, including scholars, educators, policymakers, and anyone interested in the field of comparative and international education.

Equity goes beyond mere equality. It acknowledges that individuals have different needs and challenges, and it strives to ensure that all students have equal access to quality education, regardless of their socio-economic status, gender, race, or abilities. Inclusion, on the other hand, emphasizes the value of creating safe and supportive learning environments that embrace diversity and empower every individual. It aims to dismantle barriers and provide equal opportunities for all learners.

Through a comparative lens, we examine how various education systems around the world address equity and inclusion. We analyze the policies, practices, and initiatives implemented in different countries to promote diversity and ensure access to education for marginalized groups. By highlighting both successful strategies and challenges faced by these systems, we gain valuable insights into how equity and inclusion can be effectively fostered on a global scale.

We explore case studies that showcase innovative approaches to promoting equity and inclusion in education. From inclusive classrooms that cater to students with special needs to programs that empower girls in traditionally male-dominated societies, we uncover diverse strategies that have made a significant impact. By studying these examples, we can identify best practices and draw inspiration from successful models to replicate or adapt in our own contexts.

Moreover, we analyze the role of policymakers, educators, and communities in nurturing inclusive and equitable education systems. We discuss the importance of collaboration and the need for comprehensive policies that address the diverse needs of learners. By examining the factors that contribute to successful implementation, we aim to provide practical guidance for policymakers and educators seeking to create inclusive and equitable education environments.

Ultimately, this subchapter serves as a comprehensive resource for anyone interested in understanding and promoting equity and inclusion in education. By exploring comparative insights, we hope to inspire a global dialogue and encourage the exchange of ideas and practices that can drive positive change in education systems worldwide. Together, we can create a more inclusive and equitable future for all learners, regardless of their backgrounds.

Technological Advancements and Education

In today's interconnected world, technological advancements have taken center stage in almost every aspect of our lives, including education. As the world becomes increasingly globalized, it is crucial for educational systems to adapt and integrate these advancements in order to prepare students for the challenges and opportunities of the future. This subchapter explores the role of technology in education, highlighting its impact on the field of comparative and international education.

Technology has revolutionized the way we acquire and disseminate knowledge. With the advent of the internet, information is now readily accessible to anyone with a computer or mobile device. This has leveled the playing field, allowing individuals from diverse backgrounds and geographical locations to access educational resources that were previously limited to a privileged few. From online courses to virtual libraries, technology has democratized education, enabling lifelong learning for people of all ages.

Furthermore, technology has transformed the way educators teach and students learn. Interactive whiteboards, virtual simulations, and multimedia presentations have made learning more engaging and interactive. These tools not only enhance students' understanding of complex concepts but also foster critical thinking, problem-solving, and collaboration skills. In the realm of comparative and international education, technology has facilitated cross-cultural communication and exchange, enabling students to interact with peers from different countries and gain a deeper understanding of global perspectives.

However, it is important to acknowledge that not all individuals have equal access to technology. The digital divide remains a significant challenge, particularly in developing countries and marginalized communities. To address this issue, policymakers and educators must work together to bridge this gap and ensure that everyone, regardless of their socio-economic background, has access to the necessary technology and resources.

Moreover, while technology offers numerous benefits, it also presents unique challenges. The rapid pace of technological advancements necessitates constant updating of curricula and teacher training to keep up with the emerging trends. Additionally, concerns regarding the privacy and security of students' data must be addressed to safeguard their digital identities.

In conclusion, technological advancements have had a profound impact on education, particularly in the field of comparative and international education. While technology has the potential to bridge gaps, promote inclusivity, and enhance learning outcomes, it also poses challenges that need to be addressed. By embracing technology and ensuring equitable access, we can harness its full potential to create a more diverse, interconnected, and inclusive educational landscape for everyone.

Global Collaboration and Learning Exchange

In today's interconnected world, global collaboration and learning exchange have become increasingly important in the field of education. As our societies become more diverse and interconnected, it is crucial for individuals to understand and appreciate different cultures, perspectives, and educational systems. This subchapter focuses on the significance of global collaboration and learning exchange in the context of comparative and international education.

Global collaboration refers to the process of individuals or institutions working together across borders to share knowledge, resources, and experiences. It allows for the exchange of ideas, best practices, and innovative approaches to education. Through global collaboration, educators and students can gain a broader understanding of different educational systems and cultural practices, fostering a sense of global citizenship and empathy.

One of the key benefits of global collaboration is the opportunity to learn from diverse perspectives. By engaging with educators and students from different countries and backgrounds, individuals can gain insights into alternative educational approaches and strategies. This can spark creativity and innovation, leading to the development of more inclusive and effective teaching methods.

Furthermore, global collaboration facilitates the sharing of resources and expertise. Educational institutions can partner with international counterparts to develop joint research projects, exchange faculty members, or implement cooperative programs. These collaborations not only enhance the quality of education but also promote cross-cultural understanding and dialogue.

Global collaboration also offers students the chance to engage in virtual exchange programs or study abroad experiences. By interacting with peers from different countries, students can develop intercultural competencies, such as communication skills, empathy, and adaptability. These experiences broaden their horizons and prepare them to navigate an increasingly globalized world.

In conclusion, global collaboration and learning exchange are vital components of comparative and international education. They enable individuals to understand and appreciate diversity, gain insights into alternative educational systems, and develop intercultural competencies. By embracing global collaboration, educators and students can foster a more inclusive, interconnected, and compassionate society.

Chapter 10: Conclusion

Summary of Findings

In the subchapter titled "Summary of Findings" in the book "Understanding Diversity: Comparative Insights into Global Education Systems," we delve into the key findings and conclusions derived from extensive research in the field of Comparative and International Education. This section aims to provide a concise overview of the diverse educational systems across the globe and the insights gained through comparative analysis.

The findings presented in this subchapter shed light on the multifaceted nature of education systems worldwide and highlight the importance of understanding diversity in such systems. Through a comparative lens, we explore the various educational approaches, policies, and practices adopted by different countries, allowing us to identify both commonalities and unique characteristics.

One of the key findings is the recognition that education systems across the world are shaped by cultural, historical, and socio-economic contexts. These factors play a significant role in determining the objectives, structure, and methods of education within each country. By understanding these contextual factors, policymakers and educators can design more effective and culturally responsive educational systems.

Furthermore, our research reveals that despite the diversity in educational systems, there are common challenges faced by countries globally. These challenges include issues of access, equity, quality, and relevance of education. By identifying these shared challenges, we can foster international collaboration and exchange best practices to address them effectively.

Additionally, we have found that educational systems that embrace diversity and inclusivity tend to be more successful in preparing students for the complexities of the modern world. By valuing and incorporating diverse perspectives, cultures, and languages, these systems foster greater understanding, empathy, and intercultural competence among learners.

Moreover, our research emphasizes the importance of lifelong learning and the need to adapt educational systems to meet changing societal needs. As the world rapidly evolves, education must equip individuals with the knowledge, skills, and attitudes necessary for personal and professional development.

In conclusion, the "Summary of Findings" subchapter provides a comprehensive overview of the diverse educational systems worldwide, highlighting key insights gained through comparative analysis. By understanding the contextual factors, common challenges, and the significance of diversity and inclusivity, we can work towards creating more effective and inclusive education systems globally. This summary serves as a valuable resource for policymakers, educators, researchers, and anyone interested in Comparative and International Education.

Implications for Policy and Practice

In the rapidly changing world of education, understanding diversity is crucial for policymakers and practitioners alike. The subchapter titled "Implications for Policy and Practice" in the book "Understanding Diversity: Comparative Insights into Global Education Systems" addresses the relevance of diversity in the field of comparative and international education. This subchapter aims to provide valuable insights and recommendations for policymakers, educators, and stakeholders at all levels.

One implication for policy is the need for inclusive practices in education systems worldwide. As societies become more diverse, it is essential to create inclusive policies that embrace and celebrate the differences among students. This includes ensuring equal access to quality education for all, regardless of their backgrounds, abilities, or socio-economic status. Policymakers should consider adopting inclusive curriculum frameworks, promoting cultural awareness, and providing resources for teachers to effectively address diversity in the classroom.

Another implication is the necessity of fostering intercultural competence among educators and students. In a globalized world, intercultural competence is vital for individuals to thrive in diverse environments. Policymakers should prioritize training programs for teachers to enhance their understanding of different cultures, languages, and perspectives. This will enable them to create inclusive learning environments that promote empathy, respect, and intercultural understanding among students.

Furthermore, the subchapter highlights the importance of addressing educational inequalities stemming from diversity. Policymakers should focus on closing the achievement gap between marginalized and privileged students. This can be achieved through targeted interventions such as providing additional resources to schools in disadvantaged areas, implementing affirmative action policies, and investing in early childhood education. By addressing these inequalities, societies can ensure equal opportunities for all students to succeed academically and socially.

Additionally, the subchapter emphasizes the significance of research and data collection in understanding the impact of diversity on education systems. Policymakers should invest in rigorous research to gather data on the effectiveness of diversity-related policies and practices. This will enable evidence-based decision-making and facilitate the sharing of best practices across countries and regions.

In conclusion, the subchapter "Implications for Policy and Practice" in the book "Understanding Diversity: Comparative Insights into Global Education Systems" provides valuable insights for policymakers, educators, and stakeholders in the field of comparative and international education. By embracing inclusive practices, fostering intercultural competence, addressing educational inequalities, and investing in research, education systems can better understand and respond to the challenges and opportunities arising from diversity. These implications are essential for creating equitable and inclusive education systems that prepare students for the diverse and interconnected world they will navigate.

Recommendations for Future Research

As the field of comparative and international education continues to evolve, it is crucial to identify areas that warrant further investigation. This subchapter aims to highlight key recommendations for future research in understanding diversity within global education systems.

1. Intersectionality and marginalized groups: One of the pressing concerns in comparative and international education is the need to explore the intersectionality of various forms of diversity, such as race, gender, ethnicity, socioeconomic status, and ability. Future research should examine how these intersecting identities shape educational experiences and outcomes for marginalized groups. This research can shed light on systemic barriers and inform policy interventions to promote equity and inclusion.

2. Innovative pedagogical approaches: With the rapid advancement of technology, there is a need to explore the role of innovative pedagogical approaches in addressing diversity in education. Future research should investigate the effectiveness of digital tools, virtual learning environments, and blended learning models in providing equitable educational opportunities for diverse student populations. Additionally, research should explore the impact of culturally responsive teaching practices and multicultural curricula on student engagement and achievement.

3. Policy analysis and reform: Comparative research on policies and practices that promote diversity and inclusion within education systems can provide valuable insights for policymakers and educators. Future research should analyze the effectiveness of existing policies and explore alternative approaches to dismantling systemic barriers. This includes examining policies related to inclusive education,

language policies, affirmative action, and anti-discrimination measures. Understanding the impact of these policies can inform evidence-based reforms to create more inclusive and equitable educational systems.

4. Teacher preparation and professional development: Teachers play a critical role in fostering inclusive classrooms and promoting diversity. Future research should focus on the preparation and professional development of teachers in addressing diversity. This includes investigating the impact of pre-service and in-service training on teachers' attitudes, pedagogical practices, and cultural competence. By identifying effective strategies for teacher preparation and professional development, research can contribute to enhancing the capacity of educators to meet the diverse needs of their students.

5. Longitudinal studies and comparative analysis: In order to understand the long-term impact of policies and interventions, future research should employ longitudinal studies and comparative analysis. Tracking the educational trajectories of diverse student populations over time can provide insights into the factors that contribute to their success or hinder their progress. Comparative analysis across different global education systems can further enhance our understanding of the contextual factors that influence diversity in education.

In conclusion, the field of comparative and international education has made significant strides in understanding diversity within global education systems. However, there is still much to explore and investigate. By focusing on intersectionality, innovative pedagogical approaches, policy analysis, teacher preparation, and longitudinal studies, future research can contribute to creating more inclusive and equitable educational systems around the world. This knowledge will benefit educators, policymakers, and students alike, ensuring that diversity is embraced and celebrated within educational contexts.